Marilyn Merlot and the Naked Grape

Library of Congress Cataloging in Publication Number: 2005908765
ISBN: 1-59474-099-2
Printed in China

Typeset in Centaur MT and Guardi
Designed by Karen Onorato
Cover illustration by Karen Onorato

Distributed in North America by Chronicle Books
85 Second Street
San Francisco, CA 94105

10 9 8 7 6 5 4 3 2 1

Quirk Books
215 Church Street
Philadelphia, PA 19106
www.quirkbooks.com

Marilyn Merlot and the Naked Grape

Odd Wines from Around the World

By Peter F. May

QUIRK BOOKS

PHILADELPHIA

To Joan

"Quote me more marvelous effects than those of wine. Look! When a man drinks, he is rich, everything he touches succeeds, he gains lawsuits, is happy, and helps his friends."
—Aristophanes, *The Knights* (424 BCE)

"When do we *drink* it?"
—Jack (Thomas Hayden Church), *Sideways* (2004)

Contents

Appendices

Foreword

What do we expect from the label on a bottle of wine? Obviously, it must communicate. A label that doesn't tell us what's inside the bottle fails the functionality test and inspires no confidence in the consumer.

But is it enough simply to impart necessary information about the wine? Once a label has done its duty by telling us who made the wine, where it's from, and in most cases, what grapes it contains, is there any need for more? Some wine enthusiasts would say no, perhaps pointing to the difficult example of the old-style German wine label, which flooded the would-be buyer with so much information that to read one was like drinking water from a fire hose.

But in an age when even middle-size wine shops offer the consumer a choice of hundreds or even thousands of wines, it's hard to blame the folks who market wine for coming up with tricks to make their offering stand out. The incredible diversity of wine label colors, styles, and even shapes can make a trip down a wine shop aisle feel like a visit to a very weird museum.

Every now and then, a marketing guru will christen a wine with a witty bon mot in the hope that it will make a product jump off the shelf and into your shopping cart. Real-world examples abound, from the South African Rude Girl (page 170) to the Anglo-French Fat Bastard (page 78) to the New Zealand Cat's Pee on a Gooseberry Bush (page 57).

As a wine consumer and journalist, I've long been interested in wine labels both for their aesthetic and amusement value and for their function as a

7

communications tool, creating an instant link between the producer (or its public-relations staff, anyway) and the casual wine shopper browsing in a wine shop. The more unusual the label, the more I enjoy it—even if it doesn't always inspire me to buy the wine.

But I must give way to my old friend Peter May as the ultimate guru of the unusual wine label. His popular wine label Web site (www.winelabels.org) has become the Internet's premier resource on the topic of weird and wacky wine labels from all over the world. And now I'm delighted to learn that he has brought the best of his collection to print in the form of this new book.

Whether you're a committed wine enthusiast or a novice with a sense of humor, I think you'll find this book as refreshing as a chilled glass of Mosel Riesling and as sprightly as a cool glass of sparkly Prosecco. I want a copy for my wine cellar, another for the coffee table, and perhaps a third for reading during those quiet moments in the . . . well, you know.

—Robin Garr
Louisville, Kentucky

Robin Garr is an award-winning journalist, wine writer, food critic, international wine judge, and the founder and host of www.wineloverspage.com, the world's first wine Web site. It remains unequaled to this day for its content, quality, writing team, and lively discussion forum.

Introduction

Wine should be fun. Too often it's portrayed as something complicated that you have to study and that you can get wrong. Wine is constantly being graded, discussed, and debated. For many people, ordering the "right" wine in a restaurant is so intimidating they just choose another beverage.

But wine is just grape juice that a miracle of nature has preserved by converting its sugar into alcohol. Whatever you like is the correct wine. There is no point buying a wine you do not enjoy, no matter what others say. It is you who will drink it, and you who will pay for it.

This book celebrates those who have rejected pomposity and created wines with amusing names and clever labels. These bottles cheer us when we see them on the store shelf, and they should please us when we pour them. Just because a wine has an amusing name doesn't mean the winemakers weren't deadly serious about making an excellent wine.

Guy Anderson, one half of the team responsible for Fat Bastard (page 78), told me how he maintained quality in his brand, which is now the fourth largest in the United States. He seeks out old vineyards on stony soils and rents them from farmers, paying by land area rather than, as usual, by weight of grapes. This way the farmer receives an agreed set price and has no need to overproduce. This last fact is critical for the winemaker; to make the very best wine, you need concentrated flavors from a limited number of grapes on each vine.

The innovative Charles Back showed me his family winery in Paarl, South Africa, and told me he roams over the inland mountains and valleys looking for old abandoned vineyards to purchase or lease, because old vines naturally produce fewer grapes with more intense flavors. His Goats Do Roam (page 98) is now the best-selling South African wine in the United States.

Producing a new wine is easy. The difficulty is finding a distinctive name that hasn't already been used. Every combination of natural features, ridges, woods, lanes, lakes, and hills has already been taken. Try it yourself: Invent a suitable wine name and then key it into Google. Chances are, you'll find that the wine already exists. And if you want to export your wines, the problem is compounded because you'll need to get copyright clearance in all of your destination countries.

Most of the labels in this book come from bottles I bought and drank. About ten years ago, I realized it was a shame to throw the labels away, so I began to save the most interesting and memorable ones. I was creating business Web sites and felt like doing something frivolous, so in October 1998 I started www.winelabels.org, a Web site to display my label collection. (You'll also find labels for unusual grape varieties on the site; I'm concerned about the reduced production of a large variety of grapes, so I include them to show what else is out there.)

There has never been a better time to drink wine. More good wine is made now than at any other time in history. Wine shops, Internet retailers, and mail order services offer astounding access to wines from all over the globe. Even the cheapest, while perhaps not very exciting, are usually well made and drinkable. Funny names and weird labels are not used to disguise bad wines. Indeed, if a winery makes an effort with its labels, it is likely to do the same with its wines.

So open a bottle, pour yourself a glass, dip into this book, and toast the inventiveness of the wineries, designers, and artists who produced these delightful labels.

To wine and to life, cheers!

—Peter F. May
St. Albans, England

PINOTAGE

THE DEVIL'S HIDING PLACE

A Venda Legend

Ancient law decreed that the only way to gaze upon Lake Funduzi, high up in the mountains was bent over and through your parted legs. In the ancient teachings of the Venda people it was said that strange spirits, the ditutwane dwelt in the waters of Lake Funduzi. Invisible at night, they would hunt game in the bushlands around the lake.

Many generations ago the people known as the Ba Tabadzindi had chosen to make the lush and fertile land, around the lake and dominated by huge baobab trees their home. The ditutwane made it known to the Ba Tabadzindi that they should not trespass on their hunting grounds around the sacred lake. Eventually the Ba Tabadzindi agreed to leave cattle and grain each night beside the shores of the lake for the ditutwane. The ditutwane warned that instant death would await all who saw them. Therefore it was necessary to stand with feet pointing away from the water. Gradually they increased their demands for more cattle, goats, grain and then women.

And then there came a terrible storm in the middle of the night, which lasted into the next day. The wind uprooted the mightly baobab trees and plunged them into the earth with their roots in the air. The hiding places of the ditutwane were destroyed, and the scourge was ended forever, the only reminder being the strange baobab tree which still grows upside down.

African Legend

As a youngster, bored with adult conversation at meal times, I avariciously read the ingredient lists on condiment bottles. If only my parents were able to buy African Legend back then. Every variety retells a different traditional African myth on its label. This Pinotage label relates a Venda legend that explains how the strange African baobab tree, which looks like it's upside down with its roots in the air, came to be.

Of course, the Pinotage variety has a legend of its own. It was created as a private project in the garden of Abraham Perold, South Africa's first professor of viticulture. Years later, after Perold moved away, the variety was nearly cleared away with the rest of the garden, until one of his former students rescued it. A crossing of Pinot Noir and Cinsaut (formerly known as Hermitage), Pinotage resulted in numerous prize-winning wines, but the variety became forgotten during the boycott of South African trade. Now other countries are making Pinotage as well.

Tasting Notes

This wine is medium red and quite light-bodied with cherry, banana, and berry flavors. It makes a good partner with roast springbok, kebabs, or moussaka.

Aga White

Hatten Wines	Indonesia

Few vineyards can produce one hundred vintages in seven years. Hatten Wines is the only winery on the Indonesian island of Bali making wine from grapes it grows in its own vineyards. Tropical heat means their vines are evergreens, continually producing new fruit, which allows for constant picking and multiple vintages.

Its main grape varieties are Alphonse-Lavallée, a seedless French vine used elsewhere for table grapes, and Belgia, a Muscat clone, grown on overhead trellises using small trees as supporting posts. This system shades workers and reduces the risks of diseases and sunburn on the grapes. Keeping the crop protected from the elements is a full-time operation, and workers live in houses built among the vines.

The delightful label is painted in the traditional Ubud style by Balinese painter I. Wayan Barwa and depicts a scene from the story of Bawang Putih, a poor girl whose singing enchants a prince. After many setbacks, they marry and live happily ever after.

Tasting Notes

This dry white wine, made by French-born winemaker Vincent Desplat from Belgia grapes, is pleasantly soft. Enjoy chilled with satay or on its own.

HATTEN

WINES

AGA WHITE

A delightful dry white wine
from the vineyards of Bali

Produced by PT. ARPAN BALI UTAMA
Sanur, Bali, Indonesia

750 ml   ±10.5% Alc / Vol

DEP. KES. RI. MD 100122005018

VINTAGE 1999 OESJAAR

Painting by G.P. Canitz

AMBER *Forever!*

Amber Forever!

Muratie Estate	South Africa

Muratie planted its first vines in 1685, and the old cellars don't seem to have changed in three hundred years of winemaking. Direct descendents of one of the original owners are now at the helm, but in the 1920s Muratie was owned by George Paul Canitz, a famous artist and bon viveur. Canitz built a little cottage in the vineyard, where he played cards with friends and invited attractive women he'd met in Cape Town to stay while painting them.

One of Canitz's favorite models is depicted on the label of this wine; there are several paintings of her in various states of undress in the tasting room. It was said she was his mistress, and the wine's name could be an oblique reference to *Forever Amber*, a racy romance novel by Kathleen Windsor.

Tasting Notes

Amber Forever! is a luscious, sweet, fortified wine made from large golden Hanepoot grapes (the local name for Muscat d'Alexandria). It's a honeyed drink made for sipping anytime; it's especially good on the rocks in summer and poured over vanilla ice cream for a grown-up dessert.

Les Amoureux

François Mignot	France

These two young lovers are the stars of Raymond Peynet's popular series of cartoons, "Les Amoureux de Peynet." In addition to being published around the world, the lovers' story has inspired songs, clothing lines, and countless other merchandise. And now they have a wine to call their own, courtesy of François Mignot.

Peynet drew this picture for an appropriately named Beaujolais from Saint-Amour, which is one of ten Beaujolais areas to have its own appellation. Each area, known as a *cru*, has its own distinctness, although the red wines are all made from the Gamay grape.

Saint-Amour, the most northerly and one of the smallest crus, takes its name from a Roman soldier who converted to Christianity, founded a mission, and was later canonized.

Tasting Notes

Saint-Amour wines are light bright red, with sweetly delicate red currant fruit flavors. Slightly chilled, they make a good match for a lunchtime *omelette avec fines herbes*, with a green salad and a crusty stick of bread.

Les Amoureux

Saint-Amour

Appellation Saint-Amour controlée

Tirage limité

13% vol.   Mis en bouteille par   75cl

FRANÇOIS MIGNOT

à Saint Georges de Reneins Rhône France

Peynet

CLOS DU MOULIN 69220 · PE 29

Arrogant Frog

Domaines Paul Mas	France

Aimed directly at American and UK markets, this southern French red from the well-regarded Domaines Paul Mas winery is son Jean Claude Mas's tongue-in-cheek riposte to the cool reception French wines have recently received. Showing New World thinking, it comes with the latest high-tech screw cap closure, ensuring the wine will taste as Jean Claude—who bills himself on the back label as "the humble winemaker"—intended.

Domaines Paul Mas's history dates back to 1892. Today it has four family-owned wine farms covering 150 acres (60 hectares) of vineyards on low hills along the Hérault River valley in Languedoc, in the south of France.

Tasting Notes

Ribet Red's Cabernet Sauvignon and Merlot blend is a delight. Don't be misled by the jocular name; this is a seriously good wine with a depth of complex black currant and cherry fruit flavors, some spices, and a good tannin grip. Ribet-ribet, indeed!

Bad Impersonator

Two Hands Wines	Australia

Bad Impersonator comes from a single Shiraz vineyard in Barossa Valley whose fruit produces a distinctive wine quite unlike traditional Barossa Shiraz. Owner Michael Twelftree felt the output of this vineyard didn't fit the standard blend: "It was like trying to put a square peg in a round hole." He took some home and served it to a friend, without telling him what it was. His friend's response: "I didn't know you did Pinot!"

Michael decided to bottle the new wine separately as Bad Impersonator, "because it's a bad impersonation of Barossa Shiraz." The label photo, by Don Brice, shows Michael impersonating Groucho Marx.

Michael and Richard Mintz formed Two Hands in 1999 to make the best possible Australian Shiraz–based wines; they won the award for "Best New Producer" in the 2003/2004 *Penguin Good Australian Wine Guide*.

Tasting Notes

Bad Impersonator is spicily full-bodied, with cherry and plum flavors and a sweetness that is raised by fruit acids on the finish. It suits a hearty meal such as cassoulet.

TWO HANDS
BAD IMPERSONATOR
SINGLE VINEYARD

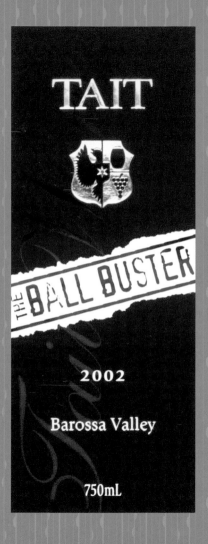

The Ball Buster

Tait Wines	Australia

Winemaker Bruno Tait first named this wine Michelle's Block, after his wife. But U.S. importers thought that name suggested something soft and elegant, quite unlike this huge, intense stallion of a wine. After tasting barrel samples, the U.S. importers requested a more appropriate name.

To Bruno and Michelle, problems are "ball busters." The wine business is full of them: tankers spilling wine, pests attacking vineyards, and so on. Renaming the wine was just another ball buster moment. After an unsuccessful night poring over a dictionary, they gave up and called the wine The Ball Buster.

"We wanted our label to reflect the style of a Tait wine, yet grab the attention of the consumer," Michelle told me. Their first vintage in 2001 produced six hundred cases, but sales (helped by a 91 rating from critic Robert Parker) increased to seven thousand cases in 2004.

Tasting Notes

This blend of 60% Shiraz, 20% Cabernet Sauvignon, and 20% Merlot, aged in American and French oak barrels for twelve months, offers sweet blackberry, licorice, smoke, and bacon-like flavors with a long, heady finish. It's a good match for sausage and mash with onion gravy.

Ballet of Angels

Sharpe Hill Vineyard	Connecticut

This beautiful label, featuring an ethereal young child with piercing eyes and an old face, came about by chance. I heard this spooky tale at the winery.

Sharpe Hill owner Catherine Vollweiler was in bed one night looking in art books for an image to use on the new wine. Giving up, she fell asleep but was later awakened by a noise. Upon switching on the light, she found that a book had fallen to the floor and opened to the picture you see on the label. Subsequent research showed that artist John Brewster Jr. was born and lived in Hampton, the town on the other side of Sharpe Hill, which is probably the one in the painting's background.

Ballet of Angels is made from a blend of grapes ("a secret," the winery told me), but the Vignoles variety is likely to be a major component. It's the most popular wine produced in New England, and it's exported to Canada and Bermuda.

Tasting Notes

This wine is crisp with a slightly oily midpalate and a pear-like nose. Light-bodied with an off-dry finish, this is an ideal wine to enjoy on its own.

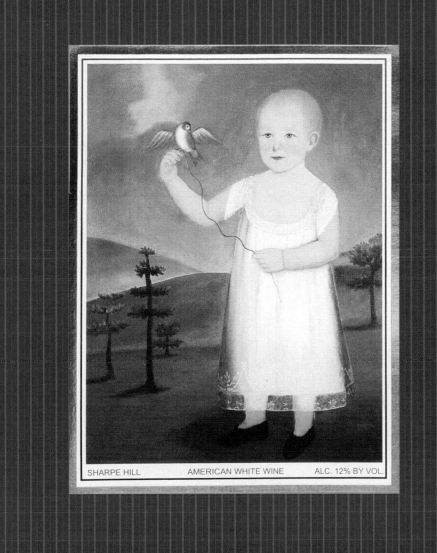

SHARPE HILL   AMERICAN WHITE WINE   ALC. 12% BY VOL.

Bear Crossing

Wine of Australia

Bear Crossing

Angove's PTY Ltd.	Australia

A road sign warns of crossing Koala Bears—clearly, this must be an Australian wine. But it's a variety—Petit Verdot—that Australia isn't famous for producing. In fact, there is very little varietal Petit Verdot made anywhere. It originated in Bordeaux and is one of five varieties allowed in that traditional blend, although nowadays only tiny amounts are grown in France. The reason is partly explained by its name, which means "little green one." This variety develops late in the season, and in Bordeaux that means it reaches full ripeness only one year in five. But when planted in the warm soil of South Australia, this variety has the perfect opportunity to show just what it is capable of—and why they still persist with it in Bordeaux.

For every bottle of Bear Crossing sold, the winemakers make a contribution to the Australian Koala Foundation to aid its educational and conservation efforts.

Tasting Notes

This Petit Verdot is a silkily rich and spicily ripe dark red wine, full of jammy black fruits and plums with violets and integrated oak tannins; it is easy and rewarding drinking.

Bearitage

| Gundlach-Bundschu Winery | California |

California's bear has stepped down from the state flag and entered the vineyard, unable to resist squeezing juice from succulent ripe grapes. In 1846, Sonoma saw the start of the Bear Flag Rebellion that briefly established California as an independent republic.

Sonoma's Gundlach-Bundschu winery celebrates that event with this wine. Its name is an amusing play on Meritage, a designation for an American blend of traditional Bordeaux grapes. But Bearitage includes California's own variety, Zinfandel, along with Cabernet Sauvignon and Merlot.

The Gundlach-Bundschu winery dates back to 1857, when Jacob Gundlach, son of a German winemaker, teamed up with Charles Bundschu to produce wine. Some 150 years later, the winery is now run by Jim and Jeff Bundschu, the farm's fifth and sixth generation vintners.

Tasting Notes

Thankfully, the bear left some grapes to be made into this wine, for Bearitage is a rich, warm red, packed with bramble berry flavors.

BEARITAGE

CALIFORNIA

RED TABLE WINE

ALC. 12.9% BY VOL.

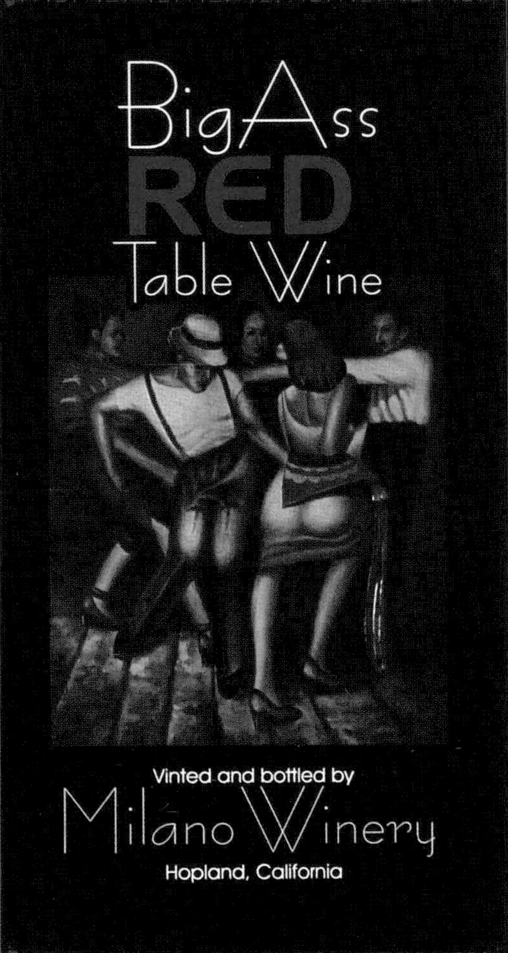

Big Ass
RED
Table Wine

Vinted and bottled by
Milano Winery
Hopland, California

Big Ass Red

Milano Family Winery	California

"I think I was the model for the picture," jokes Deanna Starr, owner of the Milano Family Winery, "but I prefer to be called *full-bodied*." Big Ass Red is one of her best sellers. "It causes lots of laughs and giggles. Many people buy it as gifts for others," she explains. "Older ladies always like it, but often when ordering they'll say something like 'Let me have one of those big ones' to avoid saying *ass*."

The winery has operated continuously since 1977 in a historic old hop kiln just south of Hopland; it was acquired by Ted and Deanna Starr in 2001. Deanna's background in chemistry (gained over twenty years of working in healthcare) has proved useful when analyzing wine to get just the right balance of components.

Tasting Notes

Big Ass Red is a Zinfandel-based blend whose precise mix changes as Deanna "makes to keep up with demand." With spicy berry fruit flavors and soft tannins, it partners with veal perfectly.

Big House Red

Ca' del Solo	California

Ca' del Solo's vineyards are planted behind the "Big House," as California's Soledad state prison is known. In this label, a guard's searchlight has just spotted knotted sheets dangling from a cell, but it's already too late—note the exiting getaway car on the left.

This bottling of Big House Red was the first premium American wine released in quantity with a screw cap. This was a brave move for Ca' del Solo, because many Americans still associate screw caps with cheap, bad wines. But this simply isn't true. Screw caps ensure that wines taste like the maker intended without being affected by cork taint. More and more fine wine makers around the world are using them; over half of New Zealand's entire output is now closed with screw caps.

Tasting Notes

While penned up, this potpourri of more than sixteen varieties harmoniously blends into soft, warm, blackberry-fruited, jammy, mouth-filling richness, with integrated tannins and a delicious, long finish.

DOONOMINAZIONE DI ORIGINE CONTROLLATA

Ca'del Solo

Big House Red

2001 CALIFORNIA RED WINE

VINTED & BOTTLED BY CA' DEL SOLO
SANTA CRUZ, CA

750 ml

PRODUCT OF U.S.A.

ALC. 13.5% BY VOL.

LE BIG
MàCon
2001

Vin de Bourgogne

CHARDONNAY

PRODUIT DE FRANCE

Le Big Mâcon

...L... Terrier & C. Collovray	France

...n, an area of low-acid calcareous soil well
...donnay wines, located smack in the middle of
...ine region.

...lled the world's favorite white grape. It grows
...ly good wines everywhere it's planted—and it
...here. It can taste crisp, dry, and minerally when
...or fatter with tropical fruit flavors when made
...k aging can add a buttery layer.

...e by Jean-Luc Terrier and Christian Collovray,
...rded the title of Burgundy Winemakers of the
Year by the renowned Gault-Millau guide.

...clean, modern-style wine, with some soft peach
...signs of oak aging on the finish. A quiche or mild
ham would match well—and goes with it better, I think, than a
McDonald's sandwich.

Blasted Church

Blasted Church	Canada

In 1929, the residents of a small town in British Columbia called Okanagan Falls decided that they needed a new church. They chose to move an unused church from an abandoned mining camp some sixteen miles away. Upon arriving at the camp, however, the work crew realized it was impossible to remove the nails that held the wooden church together without severely damaging its structure.

Their inspired idea was to loosen the nails with four sticks of dynamite. The carefully controlled blasts accomplished their goal without harming the church, apart from its spire, and the building still stands in its new home of Okanagan Falls.

This whimsical label is one of a matching series designed by Bernie Hadley-Beauregard, and it features characters involved in the move. I like how artist Monika Melnychuk has integrated the bar code and wine appellation into this picture.

Tasting Notes

This blend of Merlot and Cabernet Sauvignon is crimson and full-bodied with cassis and licorice, some oak tannins, and a dry finish. Perfect for a rib roast.

39

Bloody Good White

Ca' del Solo	California

Is it just the wine that's bloody good, or is there a deeper meaning? A fierce tiger licks his lips and grasps a glass of the wine in his paw. There's a bottle of the very same wine lying on the ground, and at bottom right is a pith helmet and notepad. There's some writing on the pad—shame we can't read it.

But let's turn the bottle, because the notepad page is stuck on the back, and the lined yellow paper makes interesting reading: ". . . astonishing full-bodied, w/good, firm backbone yet still rather fleshy, esp about the middle . . . great legs and a huge & utterly complete nose . . . excruciatingly long & dramatic finish. . . . All in all, I must admit that it really was bloody goo—" Here the handwriting ends in a scrawl. Maybe the unfortunate "great white hunter" was bloody good *eating*.

Tasting Notes

The label doesn't reveal what's in the bottle—or that Ca' del Solo is a "second label" (see Glossary, page 247) of Bonny Doon—but it's a very pleasant, full-bodied, dry wine with floral tones and a good finish. It makes a nice match with mushrooms in cream sauce, or Asian noodles.

Blue Christmas

Graceland Cellars	California

The King of Rock 'n' Roll was teamed with the king of red wine varieties for this one-thousand case, limited Christmas bottling—and the result was so successful, it sold out in days.

Graceland Cellars launched its range of Elvis Presley wine in June 2004. Sales director David Weil says, "It is a wine you can have fun with. People get pulled in by the image because they know who Elvis is. It wasn't intended as a collectible." Other labels include Presley Pinot (Noir), the King of Cabernet (Sauvignon), Jailhouse Red (Merlot), Blue Suede Chardonnay, and Shaking All Over Sauvignon Blanc.

We don't know what the King would have thought, but his manager, Colonel Tom Parker, has said that Elvis never drank wine.

Tasting Notes

The song "Blue Christmas" was one of Elvis's greatest hits, and this Napa Valley Cabernet will be a hit with festive turkey and all the seasonal trimmings.

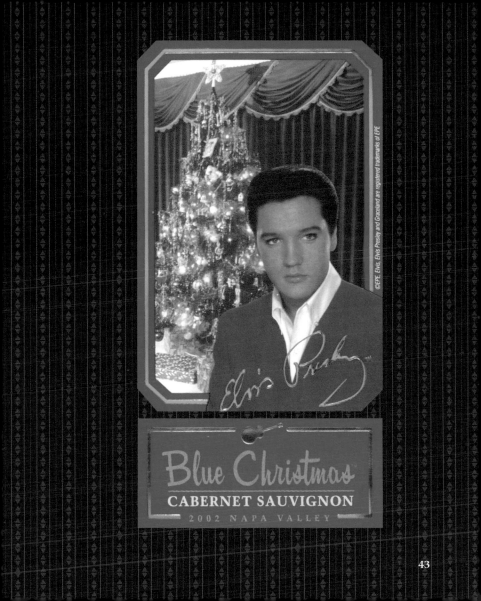

©EPE, Elvis, Elvis Presley and Graceland are registered trademarks of EPE

Elvis Presley

Blue Christmas
CABERNET SAUVIGNON
2002 NAPA VALLEY

43

BULLAMAKANKA

PREMIUM
DRY RED

750 ml

Produced and Bottled by B. Seppelt and Sons Limited
Adelaide, South Australia. E13017

WINE OF AUSTRALIA

Bullamakanka

Bullamakanka was launched in 1976 by Karl Seppelt as a riposte to criticism made by the Australian Senate Standing Committee on Trade and Commerce during their investigation into winemaking and grape growing.

Karl's cousin, Bill Seppelt, explains: "Karl became riled at accusations claiming the industry was not using Australian names for wines when, in fact, our company was using Australian names almost exclusively. He pointed out that naming wines after a little-known outback town such as Bulamakanka would not do a lot for acceptance of the product. One Senator on the panel suggested that Bulamakanka Burgundy sounded just fine to him.

"The result is the label you see," said Bill, "with a raging, well-endowed bull on the label. The spelling of the town's name has been slightly modified to Bullamakanka to exemplify Karl's ire." The back label carries a faux legend that pokes fun at government politicians of the time.

Tasting Notes

Having made its point, the Bullamakanka bull was retired long ago, so I unfortunately never had a chance to taste it.

Bull's Blood

Villány Winery	Hungary

Bull's Blood celebrates a hard-won victory from five hundred years ago. In the sixteenth century, the northern Hungarian town of Eger was besieged by an invading Turkish army. The defending soldiers fought back fiercely. So fiercely that when the Turkish Muslim soldiers saw them drinking local red wine, which stained their beards and armor, the Turks assumed the defenders' ferocity was gained by drinking the blood of bulls.

Ever since, the local red wine has been called Egri Bikaver, or Bull's Blood of Eger, and it became a popular export in the 1970s. Traditionally, the wine was made from local grape varieties, but in recent years international varieties such as Cabernet and Merlot have been included.

Nowadays, the name is used throughout Hungary for a full-bodied red wine. This example, with its striking label, comes from southwestern Hungary and is a blend of Kékfrankos, Merlot, and Cabernet Franc.

Tasting Notes

This Bull's Blood is a tasty, full-bodied, rustic wine, with plum flavors and firm tannins. It's good with braised oxtail.

VILLÁNY WINERY

BULL'S BLOOD

SZEKSZÁRD REGION

1998

DRY RED QUALITY WINE
PRODUCED AND BOTTLED BY VILLÁNY WINERY INC., VILLÁNY

75 cl ℮   PRODUCE OF HUNGARY   11,5% vol

Cacophony

Toad Hollow | California

Two semi-retired gentlemen sat on a veranda after dinner looking out over vineyards on the banks of California's Russian River. One was a leading winemaker, the other a restaurateur. Before it was time to turn in, they had decided it would be fun to make and market their own quality wines. Choosing a title for the venture was, as always, a challenge, but since one of the men was nicknamed Dr. Toad, they settled on naming their business Toad Hollow and using toad designs on their labels.

I met Dr. Toad—a.k.a. Todd Williams—in Austin, Texas, where he autographed a bottle of his Chardonnay for me, but I have chosen his colorful Cacophony label, showing the Toad crushing grapes while playing cymbals, for this book.

Tasting Notes

Cacophony is a Paso Robles Zinfandel that is bright purple-red and tastes of ripe red berries with a layer of oaky vanilla, gentle tannins, and a sweet finish. It is a perfect match for a thick, juicy homemade hamburger with all the trimmings.

Cardinal Zin

Bonny Doon Vineyard	California

It's a Cardinal Zin to be inordinately proud of this wine—or so says the ink-splattered writing of cartoonist Ralph Steadman on the back label. And not everyone appreciates its label. The state of Ohio found it offensive and banned the wine under a statute forbidding the depiction of "children or religious subjects."

The fruit for Cardinal Zin, which includes some Carignan and Mourvèdre, comes from vineyards in Mendocino and the Contra Costa County. Here, old vines grow in sandpits along the Sacramento River Delta. The sand protects vines from phylloxera; these very old ungrafted vines were planted more than one hundred years ago.

Ralph Steadman was the artist who illustrated Hunter S. Thompson's *Fear and Loathing in Las Vegas*. Cardinal Zin was his first label for Bonny Doon, and he has since drawn several more, including Ptomaine des Blagueurs (page 157).

Tasting Notes

This red wine has a beautiful deep red color, a delicious spicy nose, and complex flavors that include raspberry, plums, mint, and pepper. It's a perfect partner for jugged hare.

The CATACLYSM

RED TABLE WINE
CALIFORNIA

Cabernet Sauvignon from one of Napa's premier vineyards. Harvested on 17 October 1989, the day of the San Francisco earthquake. The traumatised vines were then chainsawed and replaced by Merlot; the ultimate in stressed vines! Hasta la vista Cabernet!

12%vol

75cle

Produced & bottled for Oddbins
by J Lohr Winery, San Jose, CA USA
Imported by Oddbins London SW19 8UG

L8942922

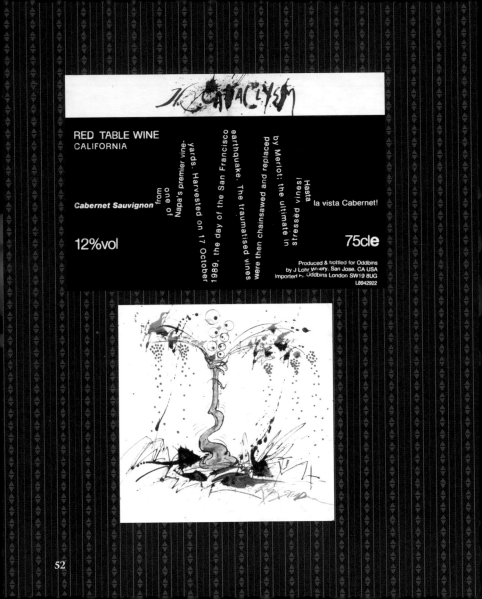

52

The Cataclysm

J. Lohr Winery	California

Some vineyards last forever. Century after century, they produce wine, replacing vines as necessary. But others have a finite life. Vines reach the end of their productive time, and encroaching towns can make housing more profitable than growing grapes. These sad occasions are sometimes marked by special labels that I cannot resist, such as Neil Ellis's 1998 Swansong, Sutter Home's 1996 End of the Vine, and this one.

During the 1980s, California saw a tremendous demand for Merlot wine. It takes four years to plant and mature vines for winemaking. But it's sometimes possible to take a shortcut by cutting existing vines back to their rootstock and grafting on others.

This Cabernet Sauvignon vineyard was harvested on October 17, 1989—the same day as the San Francisco earthquake, which is cleverly alluded to in the front label and back label cartoon by Ralph Steadman. Then the vines were chainsawed and regrafted with Merlot. Hasta la vista, Cabernet!

Tasting Notes

This wine's ripe cassis flavors are a perfect match for steak *beurre maitre d'hôtel* and *frites*.

Cat's Leap

| Freie Weingärtner Wachau | Austria |

Funny how fashions change. When this winery wanted to export its product, no one had heard of Grüner Veltliner, and Austrian wine wasn't particularly popular. So the winery registered an English language brand name and put a distinctive illustration on the front label, along with a description of what the wine tastes like.

Only a few years later, the Grüner Veltliner grape variety is in high demand. And since Austria is about the only place growing it, so is Austrian wine.

Freie Weingärtner Wachau winery is a cooperative owned by 750 grape growers whose vineyards are planted along the steep hillsides of the narrow Wachau valley, where more than 50 percent of the vines are Grüner Veltliner.

Tasting Notes

Informally called "Groovy," Grüner Veltliner offers everything white wine drinkers want. It's clean, fresh, crisp, and dry, with a citrus tang, and it is not heavily alcoholic. It's a perfect aperitif wine and great with dim sum and other Asian dishes.

Cat's Leap®

Grüner Veltliner

PRODUCE OF AUSTRIA - WACHAU VALLEY

QUALITY WINE . L"F0145299

1998

A light, crisp, dry fruity wine

Produced and bottled in Austria by
FREIE WEINGÄRTNER WACHAU
A-3601 Dürnstein

75cl e

11.5% vol

HELPING THE
SPCA®
TO PROVIDE
CREATURE
COMFORTS

Cat's pee on a Gooseberry Bush

**2004
SAUVIGNON BLANC**

750ml   NEW ZEALAND WINE   12.5% vol.

Cat's Pee on a Gooseberry Bush

Coopers Creek Vineyard	New Zealand

New Zealand makes the world's most distinctive Sauvignon Blanc— so distinctive, in fact, that many reviewers have struggled to find words to describe its amazing flavors. BBCtv's Jilly Goolden once compared it to "diving into a gooseberry bush," but it was fellow critic Oz Clarke who first coined the phrase "cat's pee on a gooseberry bush."

Coopers Creek's wine, with its bright green label and grinning cat, has been a global success, amusing everyone except the United States Bureau of Alcohol, Tobacco, and Firearms, who insisted the second word in the name be spelled "Phee." Grapes are sourced from vineyards along the eastern coast of the North Island and vinified separately. The best batches are used in the final blend.

Tasting Notes

It's almost white, with the expected cat pee and gooseberry bouquet, and a zingy, crisp, fresh taste with grassy and tropical fruit flavors. Ideal as an aperitif and with seafood.

Ceci N'est Pas un Carignan

| Bonny Doon Vineyard | California |

The name of this wine explains, "This is not Carignan," to which the response could be, "This is not your typical wine label, either." All of the legally required information for this wine is featured on the smaller back label—but what a glorious picture and name! It's a reference to Belgian surrealist Rene Magritte's 1929 *L'air et la Chanson* (*The Air and the Song*), which is a painting of a briar pipe with the words *ceci n'est pas une pipe* (*this is not a pipe*) written underneath it.

I like to think the picture also refers to another Bonny Doon wine, Le Cigare Volant (page 62). The same *cigares volants* (flying saucers) are pictured, and there is a large building, maybe the very town hall that banned them from landing in vineyards.

Tasting Notes

Despite the name, the contents *are* Carignan, with a fruity bouquet, red fruit flavors, and a meaty depth, some herbs, firm tannins, and a good finish. I enjoy this with slow-cooked braised lamb shanks.

Bonny Doon Vineyard

Ceci n'est pas
un Carignan.

59

Chile-con-Cabernet

Kingsland Wine & Spirits	Chile

Chile's vineyards are unique. Chile is the only country in the world where it is not necessary to graft vinifera vines onto American rootstock. This long, narrow South American country has the Pacific Ocean to its west and the towering peaks of the Andes Mountains along its eastern border. These barriers protected it from the dual curses of phylloxera and downy mildew that devastated the world's vineyards at the end of the 1800s. Vineyards elsewhere now require grafting and constant spraying. Luckily, just before the appearance of these maladies, Chile had stocked a nursery with cuttings of the classic vinifera varieties.

So now wine lovers frequently argue whether or not nongrafted vines are really better. If you want to decide for yourself, look for Chile-con-Cabernet or any wine produced in Chile.

Tasting Notes

Cabernet Sauvignon is Chile's major red variety, and this inexpensive example is bright garnet with soft, jammy, black fruit flavors and gentle tannins. I took the hint and enjoyed it with a spicy chili.

Le Cigare Volant

Bonny Doon Vineyard	California

This appears to be just another standard wine label, with a French chateau surrounded by vineyards. But wait! What is that hovering above the tree? Is that a death ray?!?

Cigare volant is the French term for a flying saucer. During the 1950s flying-saucer scare, the village of Chateauneuf-du-Pape feared that its famous vineyards might be damaged by visiting spacecrafts. So its village council passed an ordinance prohibiting flying saucers from landing in the vineyards. Any that did would be impounded.

You might scoff, but you cannot deny how successful that law has been. In the past fifty years, not a single flying saucer has attempted to land.

Tasting Notes

This nod to Chateauneuf-du-Pape is a blend of 40.2% Grenache, 39.5% Syrah, 13.6% Cinsaut, and 6.7% Mourvèdre. It's dark and almost opaque; there are some savory and leathery flavors, as well as black olives, and a dry, firm finish. Enjoy it with grilled filet of beef on noodles with Chinese cabbage and soy dressing.

1997

LE CIGARE VOLANT

RED WINE

CALIFORNIA

PRODUCED AND BOTTLED BY BONNY DOON VINEYARD
SANTA CRUZ, CA • U.S.A. • EARTH
PRODUCT OF U.S.A

Alc.
14.5%
Vol.

75CL

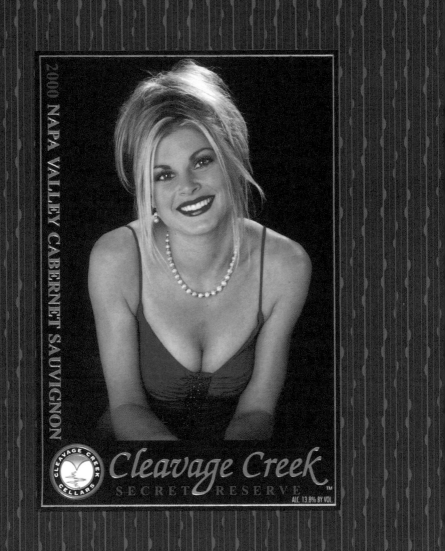

2000 NAPA VALLEY CABERNET SAUVIGNON

Cleavage Creek
SECRET RESERVE ™
CLEAVAGE CREEK CELLARS
ALC. 13.8% BY VOL.

Cleavage Creek

Cleavage Creek Cellars	California

Rounded, developed, and forward—and that's just the label.

Jeff and Barbara Conners made wine on an amateur basis for family and friends from a vineyard they'd planted at their California home. Then Barbara's grandmother was diagnosed with breast cancer. "Thanks to early detection and modern technology," says Jeff, "Barb's grandmother is a breast cancer survivor." The experience inspired them to go into the wine business as a way to combat the disease—and Cleavage Creek was born.

Wines from grapes "grown in the cleavage of California hills" were crafted to produce an initial three thousand cases. With eye-catching labels and a memorable name, five wines launched Cleavage Creek in 2003. Ten percent of proceeds are donated to the American Cancer Society. Awards followed: The Cabernet Sauvignon 2000 (pictured) won a Silver Medal at the 2004 *San Francisco Chronicle* Wine Competition. The model on the label is a Conners family friend and a cancer survivor.

Tasting Notes

This Cabernet Sauvignon has the full body you'd expect, with black currant and mint flavors, and a long finish.

Dances on Your Palate

Durney Vineyards	California

I couldn't resist this label, with its delightful title and picture. The name and dancing couple are inspired by a fifteen-foot (4.5-m) bronze sculpture by Toby Heller that overlooks the vineyards, which were first planted in 1968 by William and Dorothy Durney. The vineyards are at an altitude of 1,200–1,500 feet (350–450 m) and overlook the Cachagua region of Carmel Valley near Monterey.

I bought this 1993 vintage wine in 2001, which is quite old for a Chardonnay, but the wine was still full, fresh, complex, and good for several more years. The winery attributes the aging potential of its wines to the soil and climate. Be advised that Durney Vineyards now operates under the name Heller Estates.

Tasting Notes

This wine has yellowed with age, but its nose is fresh, as is the taste, redolent of pears, almonds, and vanilla (from oak aging), with a long, dry finish.

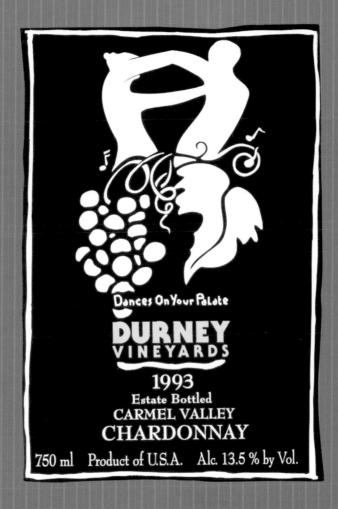

DANCING MONKEY

CHARDONNAY SEMILLON

2004

MENDOZA - ARGENTINA

Dancing Monkey

Domaine Vistalba	Argentina

This label is a nod to Aesop's fable *The Dancing Monkeys*, which tells of a group of primates trained by a prince to give a professional theatrical performance. These monkeys were so talented, in fact, that many people believed they were actually small men in costumes. One day, a courtier tossed nuts on the ground during their performance, and the monkeys stopped dancing to scramble for them—proving, of course, that the monkeys were genuine.

This Australian-inspired blend of Chardonnay and Semillon is crafted by a French company in Argentina; its true nature is a New World–style fruit-driven wine.

Tasting Notes

The blend is 60% Chardonnay and 40% Semillon hand-harvested grapes, and it has a pale straw color. A slightly lanolin nose leads into a soft front palate, with peaches and green peas, a good body, and added interest from the Semillon. Crisp, with a long finish.

The Dog's Bollocks

EastEnders	France

Dave West is a cockney market trader from London's East End who had an idea after a vacation in France. He noticed all of the travelers stocking up on duty-free French wines and spirits on their return to England. So he took a large truck, bought up quantities of booze, and parked next to Calais port, selling cases from the back.

He was so successful, he single-handedly created the "booze cruise" trip, in which Britons cross to France solely to buy cheap alcohol and return the same day. Dave and his family moved to France, where they opened a huge warehouse called EastEnders in the outskirts of Calais, next to a motorway exit. The language used is English, and prices are in pounds.

The Dog's Bollocks is EastEnders's own label. It's cockney slang for something really special that you're proud of. (Bollocks is a vulgar word for testicles; oddly, when it's used on its own, it means rubbish or nonsense.)

Tasting Notes

This unpretentious quaffer has a good, deep, garnet color, fruity flavors, a hint of sweetness, and would go well with a cockney meat pie.

The Dog's Bollocks

FRENCH RED WINE
PRODUCT OF FRANCE

75 cl

12% vol

BEL 120

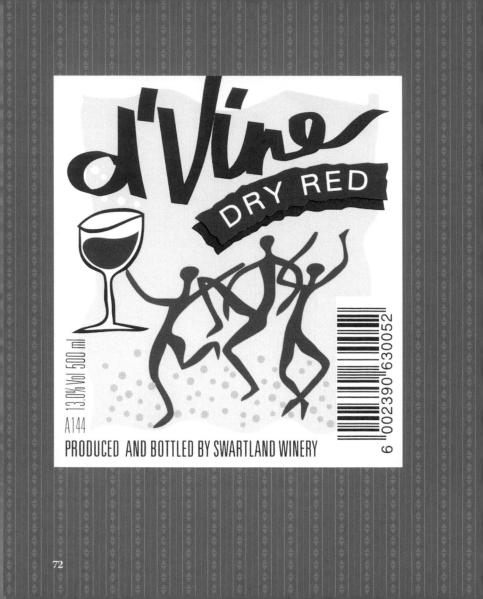

d'Vine

DRY RED

13.0% Vol 500 ml

A144

PRODUCED AND BOTTLED BY SWARTLAND WINERY

6 002390 630052

d'Vine

Swartland Winery	South Africa

This simple label and pun represent a range of lifestyle wines from Swartland Winery, which is owned by more than fifty local grape farmers. One of South Africa's upcoming wine areas, the Swartland's red soils produce excellent red wines. It gets its name from the low, dark bushes that covered the valley when the first Dutch explorers arrived (*swart* is Afrikaans for *black*). Now the valley floor is gold with grain and the hills are green with vineyards.

More than 80 percent of the winery's vineyards are planted with bush vines grown without irrigation. Cool air and sea mists from the nearby Atlantic Ocean help to temper the summer heat. Swartland Winery is the largest winery under one roof in South Africa, and it makes a wide range of wines to suit all tastes, from the tiny production premium Indalo label to the everyday nonvintage d'Vine.

Tasting Notes

D'Vine may not be divine, but it's a good value and a straightforward everyday party wine. The dry red has some good fruit and balanced tannins; it's great on its own or with a simple grill.

Dynamite

Carmenet Winery	California

Thanks to light pollution, I don't see many stars above my home near London, England. But in 1997, I was driving through the night to a business meeting at the other end of the country; in the early hours, as I passed over deserted northern moors, I could clearly see the Hale-Bopp comet.

During most of the 1990s, the Carmenet Winery commissioned an annual wine label to highlight some of the past year's events. The 1997 label shows Hale-Bopp leaving its trail across a star-scattered sky. A wolf is howling at an eclipse of the moon, and bears have again crashed through deer fences to gorge on the vineyard. One has fallen asleep with a smile on his face and a few berries on his chest. The wine gets its name from the need to blast mountain rock to make winery paths.

Tasting Notes

This full-bodied Cabernet Sauvignon had developed some rounded black currant and mint flavors and good tannins when I opened it in 2000, and would have further improved with keeping, but I enjoyed it with a Texan-sized order of KFC, barbecue beans, wedge potatoes, and a biscuit. Oh, and a healthy homemade side salad.

DYNAMITE

CABERNET SAUVIGNON

NORTH COAST
1997

ALC. 13.3% BY VOL.

EST! EST!! EST!!!
di Montefiascone

DENOMINAZIONE DI ORIGINE CONTROLLATA

Vescovo

PRODOTTO E IMBOTTIGLIATO ALL'ORIGINE DA

CANTINA DI MONTEFIASCONE

SOC. COOP. a r.l. - MONTEFIASCONE - ITALIA

750 ml e   PRODUCE OF ITALY   11,5% vol.

Est! Est!! Est!!!

Cantina di Montefiascone	Italy

The year was 1110. Bishop Johannes di Fugger was traveling from Ausberg, Germany, to Rome for the coronation of Emperor Henry V. He sent his servant, Martin, ahead with instruction to write *Est* on inns with the best wines. When the good bishop finally arrived at the small hilltop village of Montefiascone, sixty miles (96 km) from Rome, he found the words *Est! Est!! Est!!!* scrawled on the door of an inn.

The Bishop enjoyed the wine so much he moved to the town and spent the rest of his life there. His tomb can be seen in the church of St. Flavio, along with Martin's inscription:

Est. Est. Propter Nimium

Est Hic Jo. Defuk Dominus Meus Mortuus Est

Translation: "On account of too much Est Est Est my master Johannes di Fugger died here."

Tasting Notes

This pale yellow wine made by the original winery is a blend of Trebbiano and Malvasio. It has a pleasant lemony flavor and persistent dry finish, and makes a good pairing with veal and chicken dishes.

Fat Bastard

Fat Bastard Wine Company	France

British wine shipper Guy Anderson and French winemaker Thierry Boudinard were blending wines when they came across a particularly impressive batch. Guy compared it with Burgundy's famous (and expensive) Batard-Montrachet Grand-Cru Chardonnay.

Thierry had picked up his English while working in Australia. "Well matey I'll tell you zis," he replied. "It's a real fat bastard of a Chardonnay, and I zink I luurve it." Thus a jokey name was born, and the first shipment to Britain quickly sold out.

America received its first consignment of two thousand cases in 1998. It was so successful that Fat Bastard quickly became the largest selling French Chardonnay in the United States, and the range was expanded to include Shiraz, Sauvignon Blanc, and Merlot.

Tasting Notes

A funny name alone is not enough for continued success. Fat Bastard Chardonnay is an excellent wine made from low-yielding vines. It is partly oak barrel fermented, aged on the lees, and offers rich, full-bodied flavors of spicy fruit, a touch of vanilla, and refreshing lemony acidity.

THIERRY *and* GUY

FAT *bastard*
CHARDONNAY

2002

12.5% by Vol.   *bottled by*
THE FAT BASTARD WINE COMPANY   750ml

16665

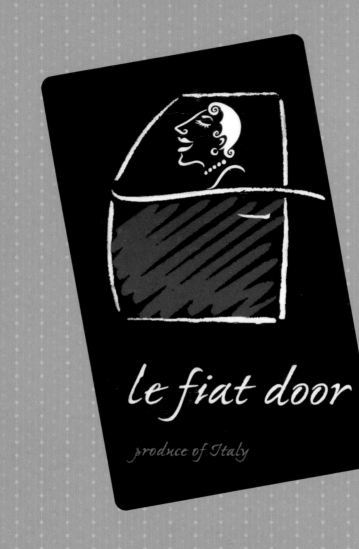

le fiat door

produce of Italy

Le Fiat Door

Casa Vinicola Carlo Botter	Italy

"The French adore Le Piat d'Or," or so claimed a heavy advertising campaign from French winemaker Le Piat that was aimed directly at the British market. In reality, most French never even had a chance to taste Le Piat d'Or, because this unexciting, bland, and suspiciously sweet wine was never actually sold in France.

Enter Le Fiat Door. This inexpensive wine from the Italian island of Sicily is much more interesting and offers a cheeky nod to Fiat, a major Italian car manufacturer. It's made from Nero d'Avola, a black grape variety found only in Sicily. But thanks to local winemakers giving some attention and care to the variety, it is coming to the attention of the international community. Vineyards as far away as Australia, California, and South Africa are now experimenting with it.

Tasting Notes

This wine is an opaque ruby-black, with a dense, chewy fullness; it has cherry and dark chocolate flavors.

Flying Pig

CPS srl	Italy

This amusing illustration emphasizes the quality price ratio of this inexpensive Sicilian red wine. The label explains, "We think you'd stand more chance of seeing a flying pig than a better wine at this price. This cherry-ripe rich red from Sicily is great with pasta, cheese, meat or on its own . . . anytime."

It's an IGT (Indicazione Geografica Tipica) wine, which is an Italian classification for basic country wines, similar to France's Vin de Pays; the constituent grape varieties aren't mentioned. But not every wine can be, or needs to be, a great wine. There's always a place for an honest glugger such as this.

Sicily was famed for its wines in antiquity. After centuries of being a vinous backwater, it is returning to the world stage, as years of vineyard investment and winemaking modernization take effect.

Tasting Notes

This wine had a bright, ruby-red color, a fruity bouquet, and soft berry flavors. I chose to appropriately partner it with roasted loin of pork.

Flying Pig

Flying Rooster Red

FLYING ROOSTER RANCH
SONOMA COAST
RED WINE

ALC. 13.8% BY VOL

2003

Flying Rooster Red

DLM Wines	California

The gallant red rooster has donned his goggles and firmly gripped the wheels. His silk scarf ripples in the slipstream as he soars out over the barn on this distinctive label. This wine's name is inspired by the vineyard's location, between California's Petaluma airport and the Rooster Run golf course.

The winery calls this its "spaghetti, pasta, and pizza red," but don't mistake it for a simple house wine. Flying Rooster Red features 80% noble Pinot Noir boosted with 10% Pinot Meunier and 10% Cabernet Sauvignon.

Tasting Notes

The delicate strawberry flavors of Pinot Noir are underscored by the slightly more earthy Pinot Meunier and supplemented by black currant tones from Cabernet. It would probably benefit from aging for a year or two—that's if you can force yourself to wait.

Le Freak

Guy Anderson Wines	France

Flush from their success with Fat Bastard (see page 78), British wine shipper Guy Anderson and French winemaker Thierry Boudinard turned their attention to cofermenting small amounts of aromatic white Viognier grapes with Shiraz. Research has shown that the Viognier helps extract color and flavor during fermentation. Although the practice originated in France's northern Rhone wineries, it is now more widespread Down Under.

Thierry didn't think Aussies should have all the fun; he'd discovered a small Shiraz vineyard with some nearby Viognier and made his first wine from the dry, hot 2003 vintage. It seemed freaky to be mixing 15% white grapes to make an individualistic red wine, but the results pleased him. The name reflects the wine's quirky origins without being too serious.

Tasting Notes

Le Freak is very dark red, floral nosed, and full-bodied, with some soft, jammy, spicy fruits and a long finish. It's great with a French beef daube.

SHIRAZ VIOGNIER 2003

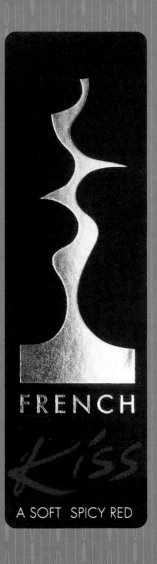

FRENCH

Kiss

A SOFT SPICY RED

French Kiss

Caves du Mont Tauch	France

The glittering metallic silver symbol catches one's attention, but the meaning of the image is revealed only by concentrating on its surroundings.

Corbières, in the Pyrenean foothills, is the most important appellation in Languedoc and the source of some of France's most interesting new wines. More than half of the red varieties planted here are Carignan, with Syrah and Grenache taking the majority of the rest. This particular blend is mostly Carignan supported with Syrah and Grenache.

Carignan's reputation for making thin, dull wine dates from the 1960s, when it was made in quantity just to get EU guaranteed subsidies. Made properly from low-yielding old vines, Carignan produces a seriously good, silky, and increasingly expensive wine, and it contributes a good deal to a blend like this.

Tasting Notes

French Kiss is dark ruby red, with a soft, perfumed nose and a berry-laden, juicy, full body that ends with a little spice on the finish. It is a good match for duck confit, stuffed cabbage, or barbecued meat dishes.

Frog's Piss

Cheers Wines & Beers	France

Frog's Piss is one of the colorful insults sometimes leveled against cheap French wines (*frog* being a colloquial English slang name for the French people, alluding to their unexplainable enthusiasm for eating frog's legs).

France and England have had a love-hate relationship over centuries, alternately fighting as enemies and as allies. But one thing the English do love about France is its wine, and buying it in France is especially appealing, since the British government taxes wine heavily while the French barely bother.

At their closest, France and England are separated by just 22 miles (35 km) of the English Channel; on the French side of the Channel are dozens of superstores packed with wines, usually at half the price they would cost in Britain. Cheers, one of the leading stores, distributes this inexpensive French wine; the name resonates with customers who buy busloads of it.

Tasting Notes

Although this wine couldn't be cheaper, the contents are pleasingly drinkable, and if put in a decanter it might be mistaken for a pricier offering.

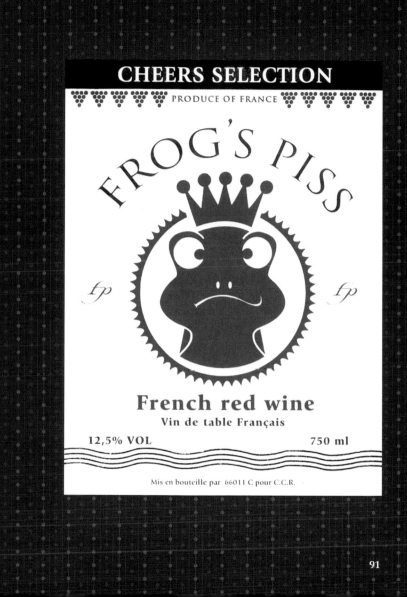

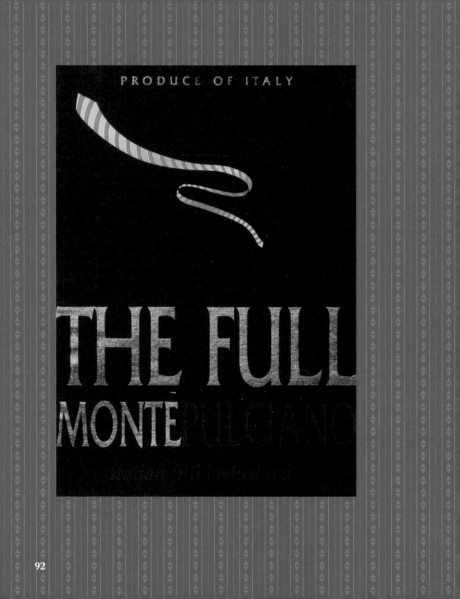

The Full Montepulciano

International Wine Services	Italy

The Full Monty was the surprise hit movie of 1997. It told the story of six unemployed steelworkers in Sheffield, England. Unable to find jobs, they formed a male striptease group to perform at women's evenings at night clubs. At the climax of the film, the lads are faced with a question: Will they have the courage to go "the full monty" and bare all?

The origin of this English phrase—meaning "everything" or "the whole lot"—is not clear. But one plausible theory is that it comes from Montague Burton, a national chain of men's outfitters in England. Any customer who purchased a suit from Montague Burton and opted to purchase a vest and spare trousers was said to be going for the full monty.

This wine has a shipper's label and makes a nice, topical play on the film's title. Montepulciano is a late-ripening red grape widely grown in central and southern Italy.

Tasting Notes

This quaffable, rounded, and well-balanced plum-tasting wine has enough acidity to stand up to pasta with tomato sauce.

Garganega

Cantina di Custoza	Italy

Everyone's doing it. Celebrities from around the world are appearing on wine labels. Movie director Francis Ford Coppola, actors Gérard Depardieu and Sam Neill, and singer Olivia Newton-John all own vineyards. And those who don't actually make wine are endorsing it—like TV chef Jamie Oliver, a.k.a. The Naked Chef, who claims that he sourced this wine.

In addition to his popular shows on The Food Network in the United States, Oliver has achieved notable success with his UK restaurant, Fifteen, which is staffed by disadvantaged youths trained by Oliver himself.

Garganega is not often seen as a varietal, but it's the same grape as used to make Italy's famous Soave wine.

Tasting Notes

I don't really believe this wine was personally sourced by Jamie, but it's a pleasant, light wine with an almond bouquet and dry, clean, refreshing lime flavors. Jamie recommends having it with "fish or veggies or with anything else you fancy." I found it a good companion for a cheeseless pizza topped with tomato, anchovies, capers, and olives.

garganega

della provincia di verona

indicazione geografica tipica

produce of italy

2001

refreshing

vibrant italian

easy drinking

Sourced by Jamie Oliver

THE WINES OF CHARLES BACK

Goat-Roti

2001

14,0% vol   SOUTH AFRICA   ℮ 0.75ℓ

Goat-Roti

Wines of Charles Back | South Africa

A braai is South Africa's equivalent of a good, old-fashioned American barbecue. The key ingredients are an open fire, plenty of meat, a lot of wine and beer, and as many friends as you can handle. I suspect that when Charles Back and his team at Fairview winery were thinking of a name for a new premium wine to accompany their best-selling Goats Do Roam (page 98), someone probably asked, "Well, what can you do with a goat?" And everyone replied, "Roast it over a braai."

And so Goat-Roti, with its picture of a goat leaping a fire, came into being. Some people (mostly French) remarked that the name sounds incredibly similar to Côte Rôtie, a French northern Rhône wine that, by another coincidence, is made from the same grapes—mostly Syrah with a little Viognier.

Tasting Notes

Goat-Roti is a delicious, powerful, rich wine with spicy flavors, a hint of smoky bacon, some refreshing acidity, and a good finish.

Goats Do Roam

Wines of Charles Back	South Africa

The wines of Charles Back are known throughout the world. But for many locals in South Africa, Back's Fairview farm is more famous for its cheeses, made from a herd of goats that live in the vineyard's tower.

These goats once escaped and began grazing on vines, picking the best and ripest grapes. They inspired the name of this southern France–style blend, which is made from the same varieties chosen by the goats.

Goats Do Roam was an immediate success in Britain and quickly became the largest-selling South African wine in the United States. The French (whom Back had already irritated by winning a number of French cheese competitions) complained that it sounded like their Côtes du Rhône wine and attempted to get the name banned. So far they have been unsuccessful. White and rosé Goats Do Roam have followed.

Tasting Notes

Goats Do Roam red is a blend of Shiraz, Cinsaut, Carignan, Mourvèdre, and South Africa's own Pinotage. It's a delicious, rich, fruity, full-bodied wine, with the taste of berry fruits, herbs, and an underlying inviting sweetness.

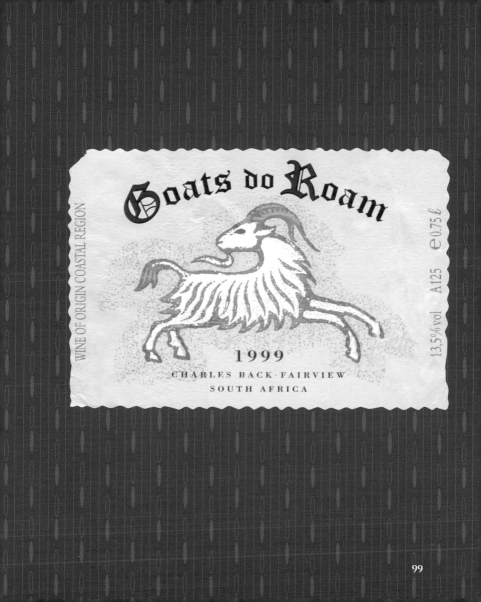

THE
GOOSEBERRY
PATCH

Sauvignon

BLANC
2003

OISLY•THÉSÉE

The Gooseberry Patch

| Confrerie de Vignerons de Oisly et Thésée | France |

Attempting to reclaim the Sauvignon Blanc crown from upstart New Zealand, this Loire valley wine states its intentions with a picture of gooseberries and a name that claims not just a bush but an entire patch of them. The label has a New World look, and it is only after a customer has picked up the bottle and turned to the back that its French origins are revealed.

Touraine, best known for its red Bourgueil and Chinon wines, is the most important region in France's Loire region. This wine is 100% Sauvignon Blanc, made from twenty-five-year-old vines harvested at the end of 2003's long, warm, dry summer. An eight-day fermentation developed the flavor that enables it to live up to the label's promise.

Tasting Notes

This wine has a light golden color and a pungent smell of apples, gooseberries, and grass. It has a sharp citrus bite, a little oiliness on the midpalate, and a long, lingering finish. It is a perfect match with fish and seafood, but (as the back label says) you should serve it chilled with anything you fancy.

Hair of the Dingo

Kingsland Wine & Spirits	Australia

With a dingo and Ayers Rock on the label, there's little doubt that this wine comes from Australia. Dingoes are native wild dogs, and a "hair of the dog"—a small amount of what you drank the previous night—is a traditional cure for a hangover. This wine is a fine example of a uniquely Australian innovation—blending a Bordeaux variety Semillon with a Burgundy variety Chardonnay.

Semillon used to be the workhorse of vineyards around the world, so popular it was simply known as the "wine grape" in Chile and the "green grape" in South Africa, where more than 90 percent of all vineyards were planted with it. But nowadays it has almost vanished, except in France, where it is the source of the luscious sweet wines of Sauternes and superb dry Graves.

Oh, and for the record: Dingoes do not bark, but they can turn their wrists and rotate their heads almost 360 degrees.

Tasting Notes

This wine is a pleasant dry white with ripe tropical fruit flavors and a medium finish.

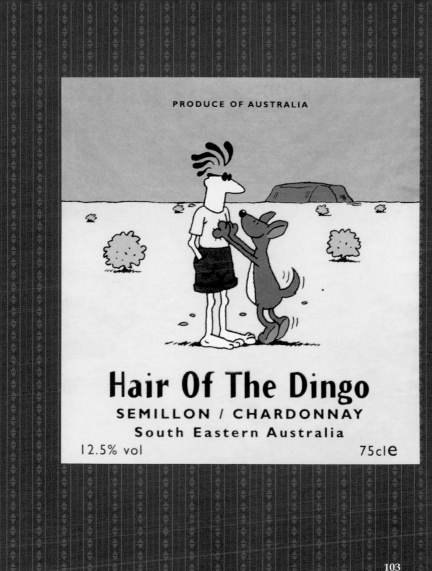

103

WM MORRISON WINES & SPIRITS MERCHANT

IDEAL WITH

FRIENDS

A WHITE TO SHARE

SAUVIGNON BLANC

Ideal with Friends

Morrison	Hungary

William Morrison's family-owned supermarket chain has been on a roll in the UK with its recent takeover of Safeway. This is one of their inexpensive brand labels, with a name that indicates the occasion it's suitable for.

I like Sauvignon Blanc, but its grassy crispness is not to everyone's taste, especially when drunk on its own, as this label suggests. I'd have thought a less sharp wine would be better suited, but the back label advises, "If your friends don't like it, change your friends," so my objection's been taken care of.

The supermarket doesn't seem to have spent much on artwork, and I bought the wine because I'd not seen a less attractive design. But maybe I've mellowed, as it doesn't seem so bad now. A Canadian company named Out of Ruins flattens wine bottles to make into serving platters, and they report that this label is their most popular offering.

Tasting Notes

The contents are from the reliable Hilltop Neszmély winery in Hungary. It's a zingy, fresh, fruity, green-tinted wine that I could keep to myself instead of sharing.

Kiwi Cuvée

Lacheteau S.A.	France

With a name like Kiwi Cuvée, it's got to be from New Zealand, right? Wrong. It seems there is nothing to prevent French producers from using the word *kiwi*, New Zealand's national symbol, on their wine labels.

When the wine made its debut in 2001, New Zealand wine producers were furious. After all, French Champagne makers had won a 1991 court case that stopped New Zealand sparkling wines from being called "Champagne." Now the French were cashing in on New Zealand's reputation for quality Sauvignon Blanc.

Stuart Smith, president of Marlborough Grape Growers Association, said the French winemakers were misleading customers and hurting sales of genuine New Zealand wine. "If we tried the same thing," he said, "we'd be in court before our feet could touch the ground." Kiwi Cuvée's producers reply that the name acknowledges their team of New Zealand winemakers who crafted the wine.

Tasting Notes

Kiwi Cuvée is a New World–style, clean, crisp, fruit-driven, green-tinged, well-balanced, and refreshingly attractive Sauvignon Blanc.

KIWI CUVÉE

2000

SAUVIGNON BLANC

VIN DE PAYS DU JARDIN DE LA FRANCE

laid back ruby

RUBY CABERNET

CO-OP RUBY CABERNET

Laid back Ruby is a wine that loves to be sipped slowly. The Ruby Cabernet is a most seductive grape, full of body behind a delicate aroma. It reflects the laid back atmosphere that is associated with California and should be enjoyed whilst relaxing with friends, ideally with a barbecue or Tex Mex banquet. Don't try to rush it! Drink within 12 months.

CUSTOMER INFORMATION

 INGREDIENTS: Grapes (Ruby Cabernet, Carnelian), Tartaric acid, Tannin, Preservatives (Sulphur dioxide, Potassium metabisulphite), Carbon dioxide, Nitrogen, Made Using: Yeast, Yeast Nutrient (Diammonium phosphate), Oak Chips, Lactic bacteria, Cleared using: Filtration, Pectinolytic enzymes, Bentonite. Closure: Cork.

! Use the DAILY guidelines for sensible drinking.
Refraining on one day should not mean excess on another.
BEFORE/DURING PREGNANCY: Most studies show that 1-2 units of alcohol once or twice a week do not cause harm in pregnancy.
DO NOT DRINK and drive, play sport or operate machinery.

	UNITS PER DAY
MEN	3-4
WOMEN	2-3

It is illegal to sell alcohol to under 18 year-olds.

9.8 UNITS OF ALCOHOL PER 75cl BOTTLE
BOTTLE HOLDS AN AVERAGE OF 6 GLASSES
90 CALORIES PER 125ml GLASS

? FREEPHONE 0800 0686 727
7 days a week
orders & info. www.co-op.co.uk

 SUITABLE FOR VEGETARIANS

L4112-0474   21:31

Laid Back Ruby

Co-operative Group	California

Wine is the only packaged foodstuff that doesn't list its ingredients—in fact, doing so is illegal in both the European Union and the United States. But Co-op, a popular supermarket chain in the United Kingdom, has defied legislation by giving detailed information about the contents of its bottles.

The company explains, "Whilst we believe that alcoholic drinks should include an ingredients list on their labels, it's not quite as simple as it might first appear. . . . Some ingredients are used but are not present in the product as sold. Yeast and finings, for example, are vital in the manufacture but are not present in the final drink." After consulting with consumers, they decided to "give an indication of how the wine is made so that our customers are kept fully informed. This includes listing the ingredients, including those which do not end up in the finished product, and the methods used to clear the wine (often of interest to vegetarians and vegans)."

Tasting Notes

This wine is a laid-back, easy-drinking wine. It is pale, clear, red, light, and bright on the palate, with some tart cranberry flavors.

The Laughing Magpie

d'Arenberg	Australia

Ruby and Alicia Osborn—the daughters of Chester Osborn, d'Arenberg's fourth-generation winemaker—called their pet kookaburras "the laughing magpies." This native Australian bird, a type of black and white kingfisher, is well known for its screeching call. When Chester crafted his first Shiraz-Viognier wine, the combination of black and white grapes reminded him of the birds and inspired the name.

Several of d'Arenberg's Shiraz vines are a hundred years old, but only in the past decade have they started planting Viognier and experimenting with the traditional Rhône practice of fermenting black grapes with a little white Viognier, which intensifies color and flavor. D'Arenburg also keeps the old method of treading grapes by feet, although these days the workers wear protective waders.

Tasting Notes

This is a fulsome, berry-rich, dark, rounded wine, with white pepper, savory depth, and a hint of smoke. Ideal with a simply roasted leg of lamb.

d'Arenberg

Established 1912

THE
LAUGHING
MAGPIE

2003

SHIRAZ
VIOGNIER

McLaren Vale

75cl   750ml

LAZY
LIZARD
SHIRAZ

Vin de Pays d'Oc

2 0 0 3

PRODUIT DE FRANCE

Mis en bouteille à F71570-084 pour *Paul Boutinot* 71570 – France

750 ml

13% vol

Lazy Lizard

| Paul Boutinot Wine Estates Inc. | France |

Lizards frequently appear on wine labels and—if you believe the stories—sometimes in the wine itself, the result of being swept up by automatic harvesting machines. For most of the year, vineyards are quiet, restful places for lizards to soak up the sun—although they'll usually dart away when visitors pass nearby.

In 1999, newspapers and animal welfare groups began reporting that mechanical harvesters were scooping lizards into grape hoppers. The next vintage, I took the opportunity to watch a harvester in action. The machine straddles and vigorously shakes a row of vines with looped nylon rods, using a conveyor belt to catch falling grape bunches. Rows vibrate for twenty feet (6 m) as it approaches, and I saw no vineyard lizards that day. Noise, vibration, and people scared all creatures away.

This Lazy Lizard contains Shiraz—and nothing else. Earlier vintages were labeled Syrah, but the Australian name for the variety is gaining dominance.

Tasting Notes

This wine begins with a violet scent and fills the glass with succulent spicy blackberry and cherry fruit flavors; it's great with shepherd's pie.

Lo Tengo

Bodega Norton SA	Argentina

This label really moves—literally. The couple's sensual Tango steps slide across the bottle, catching the eye of passersby. It's the world's first lenticular wine label and was designed specifically to work on a bottle's curve.

The label is a sheet of thin, clear, ridged plastic placed over photographs of a pair of dancers. Each side of the ridges acts as a lens; the photographs have been cut into tiny slices and reassembled so each slice is exactly behind a lens. Which photograph is seen depends on the angle it is viewed from; as the viewing angle moves, the picture changes, giving an impression of motion.

Lo Tengo (Spanish for "I have it") emphasizes its Argentinean origin by featuring the Tango, the sexy dance invented in 1850s Buenos Aires, and using Malbec, a grape variety that has had its greatest success there.

Tasting Notes

Lo Tengo Malbec—blended with a little Tempranillo and Tannat—is dark purple-red, and fruity with tobacco leaf, plums, and fleshy tannins. It's a natural with Argentine beef seared over an open charcoal fire.

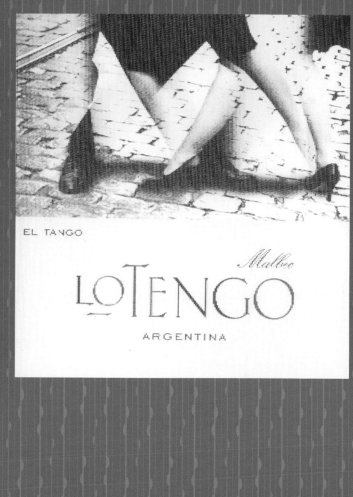

EL TANGO

LoTengo

Malbec

ARGENTINA

Love My Goat

Bully Hill Vineyards	New York

"They have my name & heritage, but they didn't get my goat," says Bully Hill's founder Walter S. Taylor on the label he painted for his most popular wine. The statement refers to his contentious past with his family's wine company. After getting sacked, Walter was restricted by a court order from using the Taylor name or history on future wines.

This didn't prevent him from striking out on his own. While local wineries were planting vinifera and cutting their wines with California juice, Bully Hill stayed loyal to native and hybrid varieties. The winery, perched overlooking Keuka Lake, has become one of the Finger Lakes' most popular destinations. Today, it welcomes large numbers of tourists, who are entertained by energetic wine tastings that include group singing and audience participation. My admitting to having visited Napa Valley resulted in a song proclaiming that Napa made car parts, not wine.

Tasting Notes

Love My Goat is a lovely, soft, fruity, medium-dry quaffing wine, made from a blend of red varieties. Ideal on its own, it also goes well with pork chops and applesauce.

Mad Dogs & Englishmen

Click Wine Group	Spain

"At twelve noon the natives swoon and no further work is done,/but mad dogs and Englishmen go out in the midday sun," sang Noël Coward in his 1932 song mocking British colonial attitudes.

Winemaker William Long, an Englishman working in Jumilla, Spain, referenced Coward when partner Guy Anderson asked him about the vintage. "It's so hot you need to be either mad or an Englishman to work here," he replied. Guy, who was responsible for Fat Bastard, recognized a good name for a wine when he heard one. The Jack Russell terrier on the label reminds William of the dog he owned as a child.

The wine is a blend of 50% Monastrell, 30% Cabernet Sauvignon, and 20% Shiraz. Monastrell is the most widely planted variety in Jumilla; it's known as Mourvèdre elsewhere and has recently become fashionable. It needs heat to show its best, and the semi-desert area of Jumilla has plenty. Says William, "2003 was hot as hell. . . . The hottest on record."

Tasting Notes

This wine is black with a purple rim and has mulberry, plum, and pepper flavors. It's a bit meaty, with tannins and a sweet uplift on the finish.

Mad dogs

& Englishmen

SHIRAZ CABERNET MONASTRELL
2 0 0 3

750ml   PRODUCE OF SPAIN   13.5% by Vol.

MAD FISH
2000
WESTERN AUSTRALIA
CABERNET SAUVIGNON MERLOT CABERNET FRANC
PRODUCE OF AUSTRALIA
14.5% VOL
750ML

MadFish

At MadFish Bay in Western Australia, the colliding tides attract plenty of large predators—which is why you'll often see small fish leaping madly from the water. This label's traditional aboriginal artwork by Maxine Fumagalli shows a water turtle, a symbol of perseverance and tolerance, surrounded by leaping fish.

MadFish's range of easy-drinking and unpretentious wines was launched in 1992. MadFish gives an Aussie polish to the traditional Bordeaux blend of Cabernet Sauvignon, Merlot, and Cabernet Franc; it uses ripe fruits to avoid the stalkiness often found in Cabernet Franc.

Tasting Notes

There's a real charm about this warm, fresh, and smooth wine, with its rounded cassis flavors and twist of blueberry on the finish. Twelve months of barrel aging has weaved its gentle magic in the background without making the wine taste of wood. It's a perfect match with tender lamb rumps in mint and balsamic vinegar crust, with baby potatoes roasted in olive oil and steamed carrot sticks.

Marge 'n Tina

Waverley Vintners	Argentina

"We girls know what we like, and that goes for our wine, too," says the back label. Two women are on a road trip, driving past cacti in an open car in a drawing that recalls the 1991 movie *Thelma & Louise*.

Waverley Vintners shipped and bottled this wine under its own label. Faced with promoting a blend of two unfashionable grape varieties from an unfashionable country, Waverley's marketing department took the cards dealt them and played a superb hand. They made word games with the varieties ("Marge" Malbec and "Tina" Tempranilla) and punned Argentina with "Marge 'n Tina."

Malbec, a minor Bordeaux variety, has become a star in Argentina, although Tempranilla (Spain's Tempranillo) hasn't performed as well.

Tasting Notes

This wine is purple colored, with some pleasant dark fruits and easy tannins.

Marge'n Tina

MENDOZA

MALBEC TEMPRANILLA

PRODUCE OF ARGENTINA

1997

13% VOL

SHIPPED & BOTTLED BY WAVERLEY VINTNERS LTD.
PERTH. U.K. BOTTLED AT NE10 0ES

75CL ℮

Marilyn Merlot™

2 0 0 1

Marilyn Merlot

Nova Wines	California

With their iconic photograph labels, Marilyn Merlot is one of the most popular wines with collectors. Not only are the wines excellent, but their value quickly appreciates as well. After just ten years, the 1995 vintage is selling at $500 a bottle, and you can buy the initial 1985 vintage for $3,500.

Marilyn Merlot was the idea of a group of friends who originally punned the famous actress's name for their homemade wine. Royalty fees support the Lee Strasberg Theater Institute and the Anna Freud Foundation in London.

This 2001 label featuring a photograph by Sam Shaw was designed by Susann Ortega. This vintage includes 3% Cabernet Sauvignon and was aged in 25 percent new oak barrels, adding complexity of flavors. The grapes were harvested during September and October 2001 from three Napa Valley vineyards, crafted by John McKay at the Napa Wine Company, and released in 2003 on Marilyn's birthday, June 1.

Tasting Notes

This leggy red offers blackberry, chocolate, oak, and smoky toast flavors. It makes a good partner with duck and game.

Naked Grape

Vignerons Merinvillois a Rieux	France

One wet night, wine shipper Dave Wright was driving home and had an idea. He would market an entire range of wines, each one being the essence of a single variety, sourced from good producers who would be happy to have their names on the label. The first Naked Grape was a Riesling from the respected German winemaker Ernst Loosen. Thanks to a simple label design and a memorable brand name, Naked Grape wines were an immediate success.

The label shown here—a Grenache and Syrah Languedoc wine—seems to contradict the original Naked Grape philosophy, since it's actually a blend of two different varieties. But it was so delicious, Dave couldn't resist it. Winemaker Lionel Arnal worked with the grape growers to ensure picking took place at the optimum time for each variety; they were vinified separately before making the final blend.

Tasting Notes

This wine has a dark garnet color, warm-scented nose, and a voluptuous fruity body with some white spice on the finish. Delightful with grilled pork chops.

Nero di Predappio

Ferlandia Predappio	Italy

Benito "Il Duce" Mussolini was born in the small town of Predappio on July 29, 1883. His Italian Fascist Party seized power in 1922, and he ruled Italy as a dictator. Seeing Hitler's Nazi army conquering Europe and tempted by easy pickings, he declared war as Hitler's ally in 1940. But his campaigns in North Africa and Greece failed, and after the Allies captured Sicily in 1943, Mussolini was deposed and imprisoned, and the new government surrendered. Then Italy was torn by fierce fighting between invading Allies and the occupying German army, who'd rescued Mussolini and made him a puppet dictator in the German zone. Il Duce was caught by Italian partisans in April 1945 and shot dead, and his body was hung by its feet in a Milan square for public vilification.

So why celebrate a dictator who brought so much death and destruction? The answer is unclear; I think this wine is mostly bought by people who regret Mussolini isn't still in charge. There are a number of shops in Predappio that celebrate the fascist era, and other winemakers offer labels featuring Hitler and Stalin.

Tasting Notes

This wine is likely to leave a bad taste in your mouth, and goes well with humble pie.

Old Fart

Paul Boutinot Wine Estates Inc.	France

Life begins at forty; the average age of vines used for Old Fart is forty-five. This wine is a hand-picked blend of 66% Grenache and 34% Syrah from the up-and-coming Côtes du Ventoux region in southern France.

In Britain (where this wine originated), it's known as Old Git, and it has become a great merchandising success, complete with T-shirts, baseball caps, talking neckties, and a sparkling wine. There's even a Web game (www.oldgitwine.com) that allows you to control an old man treading a bin of grapes. Although Old Git was changed to Old Fart for the American market, the label picture and other text remain the same.

Tasting Notes

This is a deep, purple, delicious, juicy, ripe wine, full of raspberry jammyness, hints of coffee, and soft tannins. Good on its own, and ideal with mildly spiced Indian food.

THERE REALLY IS NO SUBSTITUTE FOR
TRADITION & EXPERIENCE, JUST ASK ANY

OLD FART

For instance, they'll be quick (well, relatively)
to tell you that excellence can't be rushed,
especially when it comes to producing a superb
wine. They'll also tell you grapes from old vines
give a greater concentration of flavor and that
traditional methods are best.

But, let's be honest, when was the last time you
took any notice of what they had to say?
Which is a shame, as this time, they actually
know what they're talking about.

BE BOLD
GO FOR THE OLD

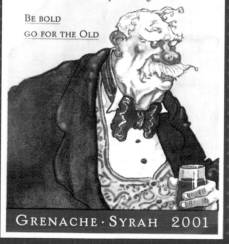

GRENACHE · SYRAH 2001

THERE REALLY IS NO SUBSTITUTE FOR
A BIT OF CLASS IN A GLASS, JUST ASK ANY

OLD TART

For instance, they'll tell you that drinking white
wine (as opposed to snowballs) adds an air of
distinction for those searching for a better class
of partner. Whilst waiting to be swept off their
stilettos (in a zippy little sports car) by a
rich Mr Right, they continue daintily sipping.

Obviously they'll enjoy something with
a 'voluptuous body' that is 'fresh, fruity and
up-front', in fact, a
wine not unlike
themselves.

**BE SMART
ENJOY THE
TART!**

Old Tart

| Paul Boutinot Wine Estates Inc. | France |

"If you're attracted to something a little more fruity, then why not grab yourself an Old Tart?" asks the back label, and plenty of people do. It's a popular gift wine in England and makes frequent appearances at parties. Old Tart is the white partner to Old Fart red wine (page 130)—but unlike her spouse, she's never made the trip to North America. In the United States, the white wine uses the Old Fart name and label.

This wine is a blend of Terret and Sauvignon Blanc. Terret is a grape widely grown for making vermouth, but as demand for those aperitifs declined, it's increasingly being used in table wines. Terret doesn't have many fans, and its vines can spontaneously produce black grapes along with the white grapes; with careful winemaking, however, this grape results in a pleasant, modern, dry, white wine.

Tasting Notes

Old Tart is a rounded dry wine with a fragrant nose, good body, and some character-giving Sauvignon raciness; it's great with spaghetti alle vongole.

The Original Z

Vinicola Cantele S.R.L.	Italy

Over the years, many people have tried to research the origins of Zinfandel. When one study reported that Zinfandel was identical to the old Italian variety Primitivo, Italian winemakers were delighted. Many printed new "Italian Zinfandel" labels to place on their existing bottles of Primitivo. But California grape growers complained, and sales of Italian Zinfandel were banned in the United States (the name wasn't allowed in Europe, either).

Wine business people are inventive, however, and along came The Original Z, an Italian Primitivo. The back label gives several reasons why it is "original," but it's careful to avoid explaining the "Z."

Dr. Carole Meredith of the University of California at Davis has since proven that Zin originated in Croatia. Primitivo is genetically identical to Zin, but is a different clone. I don't find that Italian Primitivo tastes much like California Zinfandel, but they're now planting the grape in California, so we should soon see how similar they are when made in the same place.

Tasting Notes

This was a fairly heavy, rather rustic wine with some tarry flavors under berry fruits and a tangy finish.

The Original

LIMITED RELEASE

$\mathscr{P}$ADDAROTTI

Full bodied Red Wine

ESTABLISHED 1987

PADDAGANG
VIGNERONS
BK. DE OUDE
KERKSTRAAT
TULBAGH

PADDAGANG
VIGNERONS
BOUTIQUE WINES

13,5% Vol

A166

FINE WINES SPECIALLY SELECTED
BY THE "PADDAWÊRELD" FRIENDS
PRODUCT OF THE CAPE OF GOOD HOPE, SOUTH AFRICA

750 ml

Paddarotti

Paddagang Vignerons	South Africa

Paddagang is the oldest restaurant in the town of Tulbagh, located in South Africa's wine lands, about an hour from Cape Town. It dates, say the owners, "as far back as the 1800s—give or take a century or two." The restaurant was built next to an ancient pathway used by frogs going down to the river during the mating season; its name, Paddagang, comes from the Afrikaans word for "frogs' path."

Paddagang's owners have a vineyard, and they started making wines for their restaurant at the nearby Tulbagh Winery in 1987. Their labels use pictures of padda (frogs) and froggy names. Now there are approximately half a dozen Padda wines.

This wine celebrates a visit to the Cape by the great Italian tenor Luciano Pavarotti, and shows a tuxedoed froggy counterpart giving his all, accompanied by an enthusiastic frog orchestra.

Tasting Notes

This particular Paddarotti was made of 100% Merlot (although contents can change from year to year) and offered a smooth-bodied wine with typical Merlot flavors of soft black currants backed by gentle tannins.

Perfect with Pasta

ASDA	Italy

Choosing wine to match with food is a problem for many people. Conflicting advice and the fear of "making a mistake" mean that some people give up on wine altogether. A good wine shop will always be happy to make suggestions, but plenty of wine is sold in supermarkets, where it can be hard to find knowledgeable help.

Supermarkets know this and are introducing wines specially labeled to indicate their ideal food match. Perfect with Pasta is one of a range of food-related labels produced for Asda, Wal-Mart's UK supermarket chain. It is a Montepulciano varietal from Abruzzo, on Italy's Adriatic coast.

Tasting Notes

This simple wine has an indistinct bouquet. It's light-bodied with bright cherry flavors and enough sharp acidity to make a good match with penne and a homemade tomato-based puttanesca sauce.

PERFECT WITH

Pasta

MONTEPULCIANO D'ABRUZZO

SELECTED IN ITALY FOR

Asda Wine

Il Pescatore

Ca' del Solo	California

"Ca' del Solo is an enological kingdom in exile whose ancestral lands are located at the spiritual locus of the Soledad-Piedmonte-Liguria frontiers," says Randall Grahm, the innovative winemaker at Bonny Doon who uses this label for one-off experiments. "It's a work in progress."

Il Pescatore was Grahm's take on a seafood-friendly Italian-style California wine, as broadly hinted at in this clever label by artist Chuck House. Displayed are the front label and the *rear* of the back label. This back label is magnified through the clear wine and reveals an angler hauling up a boot, shaped oddly like Italy, through a shoal of silver fish that shimmer and glint in the wine.

Tasting Notes

This white wine is a melange of Chardonnay, Pinot Meunier, Riesling, Roussanne, Pinot Blanc, and Pinot Nero. Medium-bodied and perfumed, this wine has a crispness that complements all catches—except boots.

Peter Lehmann Semillon

Peter Lehmann Wines	Australia

Anelia Pavlova's distinctive artwork has appeared on labels for Brangayne, Canonbah Bridge, and Setanta Wines. But it's her illustration for Peter Lehmann's Barossa Semillon that has stirred the most controversy. The label portrays a Queen of Clubs looking quizzically at a tall, thin wine glass held just above her bare breasts. Anelia told me, "I wanted to express the taste of the Semillon and to capture its color. Frankly, I did not expect the label to cause any controversy—it was just art. The winery liked the label, and so did the Australian public."

Exporting the wine to the United States was another matter, however, because the Bureau of Alcohol, Tobacco, and Firearms had banned nudity on wine labels. So the winery asked Anelia to cover the queen's chest. "I was more amused than anything else," said Anelia.

Anelia explained, "I drew the face with a needle on a zinc plate. I have worked many years in intaglio printmaking and have developed a technique similar to the method used by the Old French Masters. So I had to add the new clothing on the plate and print it again."

Tasting Notes

This wine has a green tinge and a citric, grassy nose. It's crisp, dry, and tangy with an oily, viscous body. Ideal with Thai fish curry.

2 0 0 3
B A R O S S A
S E M I L L O N

750mL

1 9 9 9
B A R O S S A
S E M I L L O N

PRODUCED & BOTTLED BY PETER LEHMANN WINES LTD PARA RDTANUNDA SOUTH AUSTRALIA
75cl℮ FINE WINE OF AUSTRALIA 12% VOL

THREE CHOIRS

1998
PHOENIX
ENGLISH TABLE WINE

ESTATE GROWN

Phoenix

Three Choirs Vineyards	England

Wine produced from a totally new grape variety is a rare event. That's not to say that new vines are not being bred all the time, but they have to be something very special for a winery to adopt, grow, and bring them into commercial production.

Three Choirs was the world's first Phoenix varietal label. Although the winery had released an anonymous bottling the previous year, it had been unable to openly identify either grape or vintage because the EU had not yet approved it.

Phoenix is the result of a cross between Seyval Blanc and Bacchus, both already successfully grown in southern England. Seyval Blanc is a French-American hybrid, and so Phoenix is also considered to be a hybrid; EU laws do not allow hybrids to be used for quality wine, hence the label's "table wine" classification.

Tasting Notes

There is nothing ordinary about Phoenix: It is a deliciously fruity, very dry wine with the scent of an English hedgerow, crisply packed with elderflower, nettle, and gooseberry flavors. This stunner is made for seafood and even traditional fish 'n' chips.

Pinot Express

| Benton-Lane Winery | Oregon |

Pony Express delivered letters to the West Coast, and Pinot Express delivers inexpensive, quality Pinot Noir from the west. Pinot Noir, known as the "heartbreak grape," is notoriously difficult to grow and make well, but it enchants winemakers to succeed.

Steve Girard used to make Pinot in Napa Valley but noticed that "the spiciest, most interesting Pinots are produced in cooler climates. Pinot is a special grape that does not respond well to heat." He looked for an ideal location and found it in Oregon's Willamette Valley, waiting five years before the land he wanted was available. He planted his first vines in 1989 and now has 126 acres (51 hectares) of seven different Pinot clones, from which he crafts classic single vineyard wines.

Good Pinot Noir is rarely cheap, but Benton-Lane's inexpensive entry-level Express—so named because it's the first release of the vintage—has gained plaudits.

Tasting Notes

This wine is light in color, with cherry flavors and typical Pinot silkiness. Slightly chilled, it would be perfect with salmon.

Por Pinot Express
OREGON
PINOT EXPRESS
PINOT EXPRESS
2002 Oregon
Pinot Noir
ALC. 13% BY VOL.

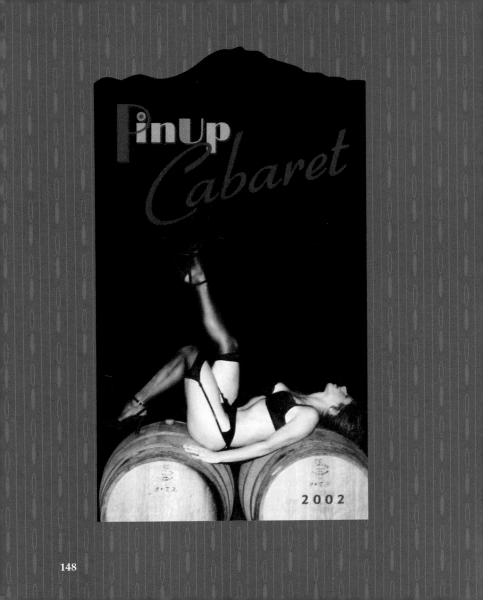

Pinup

DLM Wines	California

What weary winemaker wouldn't be inspired by finding a semi-clad beauty in his barrel cellar? This is one of a series of four pin-up labels from De La Montanya Vineyards and Winery.

DLM produces between 65 and 125 cases of each Pinup wine, and they are currently available only from the winery tasting room and through De La Montanya's wine club. Some thirty-eight hundred cases are produced annually from fifteen different varieties of estate-grown fruit, including a rare Pinot Meunier varietal and a late harvest Viognier.

Dennis De La Montanya says that the Pinup range contains some of his best wines. Artwork for the Pinup labels was approved by the notoriously prudish Bureau of Alcohol, Tobacco, and Firearms after a two month delay but no other comments. "I guess they needed the extra time to pass them around the office," he says.

Tasting Notes

Pinup Cabaret is an inspired basket-pressed blend of 50% Cabernet Sauvignon and 50% Zinfandel, offering the full-bodied elegance of Cabernet brightened by Zinfandel spiciness. Seventy cases were produced.

Pisse-Dru

Noémie Vernaux	France

Pissed—that's how I read this label when it caught my eye on a French supermarket shelf. "Pissed" is British slang for being inebriated, and the picture of jolly peasants seems to support that interpretation. In fact, Pisse-Dru is actually French for "thick piss"—the sort of boastful comment a winemaker will make about his product when he's particularly proud of it.

Pisse-Dru is a Beaujolais, a type once world-famous for easy-drinking, light, red wines, yet strangely the Gamay grape it's made from is rarely found anywhere else. Beaujolais's reputation hasn't been helped by the thin, poor, nouveau wines released in November, just weeks after harvesting. Many drinkers have been disappointed by the heavily promoted nouveau wines. They wrongly assume other Beaujolais wines are the same, and avoid them. But good Beaujolais, in particular the ones named after the villages, are a delight.

Tasting Notes

This is an ordinary, basic, "jolly" wine, and is delicious when served slightly chilled. It offers a banana nose, with light-bodied red currants, raspberries, and white pepper flavors; Pisse-Dru just asks to be matched with paté.

BEAUJOLAIS
APPELLATION BEAUJOLAIS CONTRÔLÉE

PISSE-DRU

750 ml ℮   12% vol.

ÉLEVÉ ET MIS EN BOUTEILLE EN RÉGION DE PRODUCTION PAR NOÉMIE VERNAUX, A 21 200, FRANCE

FRANCE

PKNT

CARMENERE
Central Valley / Chile

13.5% vol.

75 cl e

PKNT

Terraustral	Chile

When spoken, the name of this wine sounds like *piquant*, or even *picante*, the Chilean word for spicy. Although I suspect some might assume the bottle has a hot pepper inside, what it really contains is Carmenère, a rare grape variety similar to Merlot that was once grown in Bordeaux and is now found almost exclusively in Chile.

Legend says that when buyers went to Chile in the '90s looking to satisfy America's insatiable demand for Merlot, they couldn't find any. Growers shook their heads. "Someone must have Merlot," exploded one buyer. "We're prepared to pay top dollar and take all you have." The growers looked at each other then exclaimed, "Oh, Merlot! You want Merlot? We have Merlot," and then many Chilean bottles labeled as Merlot actually contained Carmenère. The varieties do look alike and have been planted together in vineyards. Carmenère has only recently been correctly identified, and Chile allowed its varietal labeling only since 1998.

Tasting Notes

PKNT is almost black in the glass. A powerful blackberry bouquet presages rich, silky flavors encompassing black currants, ripe plums, ground spices, and coffee grounds with fruity sweetness.

Le Prince

| Desire Delatour | France |

This stylish playing card label left me wondering why the third court card is always a Jack instead of a prince or princess. And what does *Jack* mean, anyway?

A little research reveals that playing cards have inherited a tradition of two powerful figures, portrayed as a King and Queen, plus their servant. Early cards called the servant a *Knave*, shortened to *Kn* on corners, but since this was easily confused with the *K* of *King*, it was changed to *Jack*. You might also wonder why royals would want a knave—a rogue, rascal, or villain—for a servant. But over the centuries, this word has undergone a change of meaning; etymologists believe that *knave* originally just meant *boy*, as did *Jack*. French playing cards avoid the issue altogether. They just use *Valet*.

Tasting Notes

This is a very cheap, basic, French table wine with no pretensions, but someone got imaginative by featuring this cheerful prince. The contents are also pleasing. It's a light-bodied pale red wine with a cherry perfume and flavors.

LE PRINCE

ROUGE

Vin de Table de France

SYRAH

1996

Vin de Pays d'Oc   Product of France

ALC 12.5% VOL.

75cl e

1996

Domaine des Blagueurs

Bottled by Les Celliers Jean D'Alibert   F1116 Rieux Minervois, France

Ptomaine des Blagueurs

Bonny Doon Vineyards	France

When Bonny Doon's Randall Grahm first traveled from California to France to make wine from some of his favorite varieties, he noted, "We have embarked upon a great European adventure that will prove to be either as visionary as the Marshall Plan or as utterly misguided as *Plan 9 from Outer Space*." He had no idea then what a nightmare French bureaucracy could be. His experiences were such that he labeled the results of his European adventures under the scathing name Ptomaine des Blagueurs. (*Blagueurs* are people who talk nonsense, and *Ptomaine* is the poisonous vapor from a corpse.)

This Ralph Steadman illustration shows "a certain genre of snaky, slithery, slimy, smarmy, sebaceous sommelier and the insufferable *snobbisme* associated therewith." Later bottlings used the word *domaine* instead of *ptomaine*, for reasons unknown. Perhaps Grahm's dislike of the French had mellowed.

Tasting Notes

This unfiltered wine is a blend of Syrah from Costières de Nîmes and Minervois, fermented in the local manner with a little white Viognier. It's very dark, with powerful plum fruit, chocolate, and spice flavors, and backed with firm tannins.

Rasteau

M. Chapoutier	France

Customers sometimes complain about damaged labels on Chapoutier's wines. But the labels are not faulty; their rough surface is caused by Braille embossing. Chapoutier was the first—and remains one of very few—wineries that prints its labels in Braille. When asked why he did so, Michel Chapoutier replied, "Why not?"

Chapoutier decided that blind and partially sighted people needed a means of identifying bottles of wine in order to fully appreciate them. The Valentin Hauy Association for visually impaired people helped translate all the necessary information into Braille, including the wine's name, appellation, color, and vintage, as well as the producer's name and location. Modifying a typography machine to print Braille took more than a year of research and refinement.

Now Chapoutier's entire annual production of two million bottles are labeled in Braille, and the winery invites other wineries to share its research and methodology.

Tasting Notes

This is a full-bodied Grenache, with peppery fruit flavors and a hint of black olives on the finish. Great with a slow-cooked ratatouille stew.

Rasteau

CÔTES-DU-RHÔNE-VILLAGES

APPELLATION CÔTES-DU-RHÔNE-VILLAGES CONTRÔLÉE

mis en bouteille par

M. CHAPOUTIER

26600 TAIN (FRANCE)

PRODUIT DE FRANCE
PRODUCE OF FRANCE

750 ml
RED WINE
VIN ROUGE

1996
75 cl
13 % alc./vol.

Recall Red

| Milano Family Winery | California |

Recall Red was inspired by California's October 2003 gubernatorial recall election, in which Governor Gray Davis lost his office a year after he'd been reelected. The wine was popular during the run-up to the recall election and continued selling well for years afterward. Its label was cleverly designed to match all political leanings. The "no clowns" logo over the state capital on the map of California could be read as, "We don't want any clowns coming to Sacramento!" or "Get the clowns out of Sacramento!"

Owner-winemaker Deanna Starr told me, "Recall Red is on display in a recall election memorabilia collection at Sacramento's California State History Museum. It still sells at charity auctions. One bottle recently sold for $275, and the highest ever went for $1,000."

The winner of the recall election, actor Arnold Schwarzenegger, owns several bottles.

Tasting Notes

Recall Red is a blend of Cabernet, Merlot, Zinfandel, and Petite Sirah. It offers a pleasing fruity wine with some spiciness and a hint of sweetness. Good for sipping on its own, or with a mild curry.

Rex Goliath! HRM

HRM Rex-Goliath Wines	California

I learned from experience that everything is bigger in Texas, but in my travels I never came across a giant chicken. It's true that the portions at KFC in the States were bigger than back home, but I could still manage to lift the drumsticks.

But apparently Texas was home to a forty-seven-pound (21-kg) rooster at the beginning of the twentieth century. There was no television and few other entertainment options back then, so "The World's Largest Rooster" became a star draw at the circus. His handlers promoted him as "His Royal Majesty Rex Goliath," and this label is based on the banner the circus hung above his roost.

The brand was developed in reaction to the inroads Australian wines, such as Yellowtail, have made in the U.S. market. The competitively priced Rex Goliath sold one hundred and eighty thousand cases in its first fourteen months and gained export sales.

Tasting Notes

This nonvintage (or "free range") Cabernet Sauvignon has jammy plums and raspberries on the nose, which carry through to the palate and are joined by hints of dark chocolate and soft tannins.

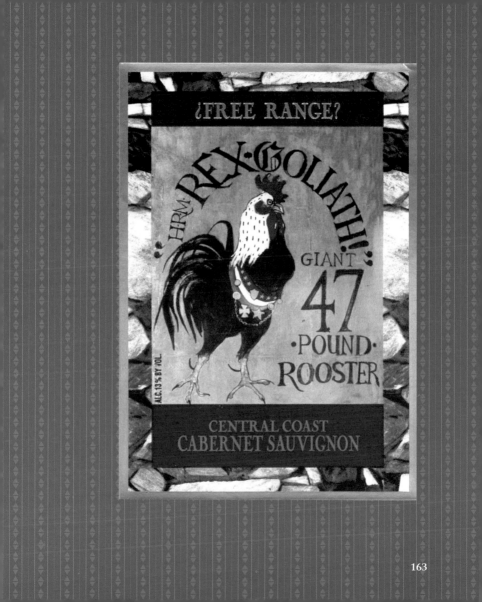

SAKONNET

RHODE

RHODE ISLAND

RED

2002

Rhode Island Red

Sakonnet Vineyards	Rhode Island

What else could Sakonnet Vineyards call this red blend? Founded in 1975, the vineyard is Rhode Island's oldest winery; it farms fifty acres (20 hectares) of mostly vinifera varieties, including Chardonnay, Gewürztraminer, Pinot Noir, and Cabernet Franc. It annually produces more than thirty thousand cases from estate-grown and bought-in fruit.

Christian Butzke, director of winemaking at Sakonnet, invited Rhode Island School of Design's Graphic Design Graduate Student Studio to create the 2002 label. Cavan Huang, Scott Thorpe, Susie Nielsen, and Peter Freedman came up with this eye-catcher, and won a $1,000 prize donated by winery owners Susan and Earl Samson. The wine, with its new label, was released in time for the fiftieth anniversary of Rhode Island's adoption of the Red Hen as state bird in 1954.

Tasting Notes

Rhode Island Red is an interesting blend of 50% Chancellor, 25% Cabernet Franc, and 25% Lemberger. It is dark red and full-bodied with a tang from the Cabernet and a good depth of blueberry fruit flavors. It makes a good match for roast chicken with mashed sweet potatoes and corn.

Ridge

| Ridge Vineyards | California |

I am often asked to name my favorite labels. It's a difficult question to answer, but on reflection, the labels from California's Ridge Vineyards take the prize. The company uses a label that wraps around the bottle and contains both the front and back label information. The standard label design has used the same typeface and colors for more than three decades.

The label tells you all the information you need. At the simplest level, it clearly identifies the winery, region, variety, vineyard, and vintage. Ridge often makes "field blends" from a vineyard planted with several different varieties; although not required to do so, Ridge shows the percentage of each variety. There is a dated note from the winemaker (PD = Paul Draper), and general information about the winery.

Ridge labels are consumer-friendly design classics, and their wine is superb.

Tasting Notes

This particular wine is a rare ATP bottling usually available only to Advanced Tasting Program (see Glossary, page 247) members. It had a soft, perfumed nose and was a beautifully balanced, smooth, complex mix of spice, berries, and pepper. Ideal with a plain broiled steak.

93 Zinfandel, Lytton Estate, bottled March 95
At the end of September, we harvested three of the Estate's six hills. As the wines developed in depth and intensity, they were set aside for the Advance Tasting Program. Combined with late-picked grapes from House Hill, they have become a beautifully-structured wine with concentrated fruit and lively spice. Substantial tannin ensures that this rich, claret-like wine will continue to develop over the next five to eight years.   PD (1/95)

Since 1962, Ridge has championed single-vineyard winemaking, exploring California in search of great vineyards where climate, soil, and varietal are ideally matched. Unlike other alcoholic beverages, fine wine, when made traditionally, is the result of a natural process. Using traditional methods and minimal handling, we strive to produce the highest quality wines from superior and distinctive fruit. We are proud that our three decades are an integral part of California's winemaking history. For information on the wines, or visiting us at our Monte Bello or Lytton Springs Wineries, call (408) 867-3233.

RIDGE
CALIFORNIA
ZINFANDEL
LYTTON ESTATE
1993

GRAPES: 88% ZINFANDEL, 12% PETITE SIRAH
DRY CREEK, SONOMA   ALCOHOL 15.1% BY VOLUME
PRODUCED AND BOTTLED BY RIDGE VINEYARDS   BW 4488
17100 MONTE BELLO ROAD, BOX 1810, CUPERTINO, CA 95015

RUDE BOY
C H A R D O N N A Y

Rude Boy

Western Wines	South Africa

This rude boy likes nothing more than chillin' out. Put him in a fridge for thirty minutes, and when he's ready for you, he'll take off his shorts. The label is printed with a temperature sensitive ink that, when cold, reveals what is underneath.

The wine inside is Bridget Jones's favorite kind—Chardonnay. Maybe Rude Boy is the reason why. Chardonnay originated in Burgundy and is now grown successfully almost everywhere, making consistently good white wines. Winemakers like it because it is a fairly bland grape that can be crafted in any style, and consumers love its sheer drinkability.

Rude Boy's partner, Rude Girl, is on the next page.

Tasting Notes

This fresh, fruity wine has some tropical fruit flavors and is good for drinking on its own, or with salads, fish, or chicken.

Rude Girl

Western Wines	South Africa

Whenever my supermarket has Rude Girl in stock, I always see customers cradling the bottles and sometimes breathing on them.

It's an odd sight, but they're actually testing the label. The demurely dressed woman on the label is telling us she's cold, and the bottle needs to be warmed a bit more before its contents are ready to drink. When the bottle does reach the correct serving temperature, the little black dress fades away, and we see why she's called rude.

This fun use of heat-sensitive inks caused this inexpensive wine to quickly sell out. It's a bulk Shiraz from South Africa, bottled and labeled in England by innovative shippers Western Wines.

Tasting Notes

Shiraz plantings are growing fast in the Cape, because hot weather suits the variety. This wine is probably from young vines, but delivers a purple, fruity, full-bodied wine with some tangy spices. It makes a good pairing with spaghetti and meatballs.

RUDE GIRL
SHIRAZ

"UNE MAISON DE TRADITION"
SAINT-AMOUR, œuvre originale zak & landau

SAINT-AMOUR

appellation saint-amour contrôlée

Saint-Amour

Maison Coquard	France

Beaujolais, with millions of bottles of unsold wine, has been having a bad time recently. A glut of California wines, the popularity of Australian wines, and a rise in the value of the Euro have all contributed to the decline of Beaujolais. "It's a challenge," admits winemaker Christophe Coquard. But he is quietly confident his wine retail experience in England and work at top wineries in South Africa, New Zealand, and France will give him an edge when it comes to marketing Beaujolais. Christophe was born in the region, where his parents own vineyards, and so for him Beaujolais was the only choice for a new wine business.

Working with Australian winemaker Jeremy Dixon, the two men use New World techniques "while retaining respect for the notion of *terroir*, which is the essence of fine French wines."

Christophe commissioned artists Zak & Landau to design nine labels based on a house. I have selected Saint-Amour, which contains romantic hearts.

Tasting Notes

"Une Maison de Tradition" Saint-Amour is bright red, with attractively drinkable soft, red berry flavors. It's great with quiche.

Salt Spring Vineyards

Salt Spring Vineyards	Canada

In the fall of 2002, Salt Spring Vineyards was the only winery on Salt Spring Island (just off America's West Coast, between Vancouver and Seattle). It enjoyed this distinction for just half an hour, until a neighboring vineyard received a similar license. A month later, in October 2002, Salt Spring started picking its grapes. This label, designed by Marc Doherty, uses a delightful painting of Eartha, the earth goddess, by Luc Latulippe. She is bestowing her bounty of fruits, vegetables, animals, fish, bread, cheese, and wines. Visitors are shown arriving by air and sea to enjoy the island's produce and scenery.

Pinot Gris, also known as Pinot Grigio, is a white grape whose skin goes an intriguing pink when ripe. This mutation of the black Pinot Noir makes classic wines in Alsace and popular fruity quaffers in Italy. It's also gaining ground in Canada.

Tasting Notes

This wine has honeyed tones, some sweetness, and pear flavors. It's balanced by crisp fruit acids and makes a good match for locally caught seafood.

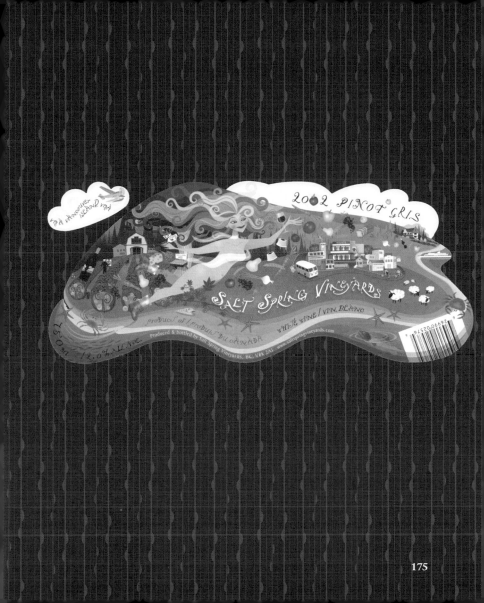

Scraping the Barrel

TEMPRANILLO

OAK AGED

Utiel Requena
Denominacion de Origen

12.5% vol

SHIPPED AND BOTTLED BY
BARBER KINGSLAND, M44 6BD, UK

75cl℮

Scraping the Barrel

Kingsland Wine & Spirits	Spain

It's a dirty, unpleasant winery chore to clean out the tartrates, dead yeast, seeds, pulp, and other sediments that cling to the inside of barrels after the winemaking process. But a barrel is easier to access than fermentation tanks, which have tiny hatches that only small people can climb through.

"Scraping the barrel" also implies using leftovers or dregs, but that's not an accurate description of this enjoyable wine. It comes from the hills of Utile-Requiena near Valencia and is made from Spain's great Tempranillo, the red grape of Rioja. Tempranillo is an early ripening grape, as its name acknowledges (*temprano* in Spanish means *early*). With many advantages—reliable, fruity, and low on tannins and acids— winemakers around the world are trialing the grape, and we'll be seeing more Tempranillo on the shelves in years to come.

Tasting Notes

This wine is an easy-quaffing, fruity red, with soft strawberry and plum flavors that match well with meatloaf or stew. The back label even suggests drinking this Tempranillo with French fries and gravy.

Screw Kappa Napa

Three Loose Screws Wine Company	California

American consumers remain wary of screw-cap closures for quality wine, but a new company is out to change that attitude. The Three Loose Screws Company was founded by three members of the historic winery-owning Sebastiani family. Don Sebastiani jokes that the name refers "less to the bottle closure and more to the proprietors of the company."

The Screw Kappa Napa wine's name proudly proclaims both the origin of the wine and its closure. Don says Screw Kappa Napa was "the single largest bottling of Napa Valley Cabernet Sauvignon in screw caps. We think screw caps are the way to go from every aspect of brand marketing, wine quality, image, and ease of use."

Tasting Notes

This Cabernet Sauvignon offers raspberry and coffee flavors backed by vanilla and tannins from oak aging. It partners well with grilled lamb leg steaks.

SCREW
KAPPA
NAPA

2002
NAPA VALLEY

CABERNET SAUVIGNON

750 ml
Alc. 13.5% By Vol

Le
secret
de
Frère
Nonenque

Abbaye de Valmagne
Mis en bouteille à la propriété

Le Secret de Frère Nonenque

Abbaye de Valmagne	France

This wine's name translates as "the secret of Brother Nonenque," who in 1575 was winemaker at the Abbey of Valmage in the Herault district of southern France. Cistercian monks first planted vineyards in this region in the twelfth century. Following the French revolution, the state took over and sold the abbey, which was acquired by the family of Phillippe d'Allaines, the current owner, in 1838.

So what is Brother Nonenque's secret? It's the varieties that make up the blend. Brother Nonenque (pictured on this label) made his red wines from a now mostly vanished grape called Morrastel.

The winery recently decided to recreate wines of Brother Nonenque's era and managed to find some surviving examples of the variety elsewhere. Abbaye de Valmagne propagated these cuttings for their vineyard. This is the first modern vintage to contain Morrastel; there's 20% of it blended with Grenache and Carignan.

Tasting Notes

The wine is ruby red; it is rich with the warmth of southern France and flavors that remind me of the wild-herb-covered hills of the region. The ghost of Brother Nonenque is surely smiling.

Sex

L. Mawby Vineyards	Michigan

Submitting wine labels for approval to the U.S. Alcohol and Tobacco Tax Trade Bureau (TTB) is an annual chore for American wineries. As Larry Mawby filled in the forms for his winery, he mischievously included an application to rename his pink sparkling wine from Rosé to Sex. "I didn't expect it to get through," he told me. "I did it for a laugh." But to his surprise, the usually prudish TTB didn't object. When Larry started shipping wines with the new label, he found sales shot up. "We kept the poem from the old label," he grins, "and now people find a different meaning in it."

Tasting Notes

This traditional blend of Pinot Noir and Chardonnay has a beautiful pale pink color, with a good flow of bubbles and a dry, refreshing, tangy strawberry taste. Makes a great partner with strawberries lightly dusted with cracked black pepper.

M. LawReNCE

In a pale fresh stream
slowly rising bubbles pour
down our throat & whisper
softly the secret sounds
of that pink mystery.

M. Lawrence sparkling wines are hand-
crafted in small batches by L. Mawby,
using fine winegrapes from select
vineyards. The bubbles in these seriously
fun wines are produced by fermentation
in the cuve close method.
For more information about our wines,
please visit our website:
www.lmawby.com

M. LawReNCE

SEX

SPARKLING   WINE

BRUT   **2524** OF 2574 BOTTLES
ROSE   BATCH #8

ALCOHOL 12% BY VOLUME   750 ML

Fair Dinkum Winery
FAIR DINKUM
SHEILA'S CHARDONNAY
ALTHOUGH BRUCE DID HELP (A BIT)
Produce of Australia
NO SHEEP WERE HARMED IN THE MAKING OF THIS FINE WINE

Sheila's Chardonnay

Capricorn Wines	Australia

This label shows cheerful Sheila and friend standing outside the Fair Dinkum winery, though I've not been able to find any record of such a place anywhere in Australia. I rather suspect that the winery, Sheila, and hubby Bruce (who helped "a bit") are the figments of a clever marketer's imagination.

Clearly, this label is meant to evoke Australia (note the hat with dangling corks). Bruce and Sheila are archetypal Australian names immortalized by Monty Python sketches that scoffed at Australian wine. Of course, it's the Australians who are laughing now, as their wines continue to conquer world markets. A little research revealed that this wine was bottled in France for a UK-based company.

Tasting Notes

This wine is a pleasant, simple Chardonnay, a little citrussy with a fat, creamy middle and a good finish; it goes well with chicken in a cream sauce. I was pleased to read that "no sheep were harmed during the making of this fine wine."

Skuttlebutt

Stella Bella Wines	Western Australia

Scuttlebutts were the office water coolers of old wooden sailing ships, where people would gather to quench their thirst, gossip, and exchange rumors. It's a portmanteau word formed by combining *scuttle* (the sailor's name for an opening or hatch) and *butt* (a large cask). Thus it was a barrel with its top opened to allow access to drinking water. The term is still in nautical use for a drinking fountain.

This Skuttlebutt tap is dispensing purple wine, and a closer look reveals faces in the froth. Produced by the Stella Bella winery in the remote Margaret River area of Western Australia, Skuttlebutt blends come in red and white versions (Sauvignon Blanc, Semillon, and Chardonnay) and will be soon joined by a rosé made from Shiraz and Merlot.

Tasting Notes

This red blend of 40% Cabernet Sauvignon, 40% Shiraz, and 20% Merlot has a garnet color with full-bodied rich berry and spice flavors. Teams well with rabbit stew.

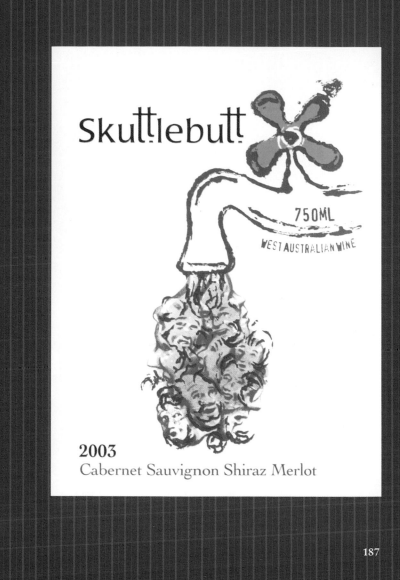

SMOKING PARROT

Sauvignon Blanc

2001

Vin de Pays du Jardin de la FRANCE

Ralph STEADman 2002

SFC E77412/001

Smoking Parrot

Oddbins Limited	France

Smoking Parrot is a pun on a much more famous wine name—have you figured it out? The answer follows below.

Innovative UK wine shop chain Oddbins sourced this wine from the Loire region. Smoking Parrot is an excellent Sauvignon, as good as the world-famous Sauvignons of that region. But European Union wine laws forbid Oddbins from putting the Loire name on the bottle, and you'd need a textbook to understand that "Vin de Pays de Jardin de la France" is a reference to this region. So an eye-catching cartoon from Ralph Steadman and a punning name is used to tip off shelf browsers that the contents of this bottle are worth consideration.

The pun's solution? A common parrot name is "Polly," and the word *fumé* means *smoking* in French, so we get *polly fumé*, which is about as close as a non-French speaker can get to Pouilly-Fumé, the classic Sauvignon Blanc from the Loire.

Tasting Notes

This pale wine is clean, fresh, and tangy, with tones of nettles and gooseberries and a hint of smoke.

Sonoma Beach Zinfandel

Stu Pedasso Cellars	California

Stuart "Stu" Pedasso's move into organic farming is the talk of Sonoma. Locals tell me he bought bullfrogs to eat vineyard pests, but they preferred to spend their time mating; soon there were thousands of them causing many complaints from neighbors about their noise. Unable to use poisons against the frogs because of his organic status, Stu introduced fifty Florida alligators. While the alligators lazed in the pond snacking on frogs, deer were eating all the grapes, so Stu bought twenty-five Indonesian monitor lizards.

"These ten-foot (3-m) long lizards are the best pest killers I've ever seen," said Stu. "When one of these throwbacks from the dinosaurs gets hold of a jackrabbit or a deer, it's not a pretty picture." Stu hopes they'll also take care of the alligators and any remaining frogs. After all, it seems these lizards will eat anything. Tours of Stu's vineyards are strictly by appointment only. If the gate is closed, enter at your peril.

Tasting Notes

Vineyard problems haven't prevented Stu from making this most drinkable Zinfandel from the Sonoma Beach (careful how you say it) appellation. It's dark red, perfumed, and packed with peppery and spicy flavors, and it goes very well with steak.

Stu Pedasso
Cellars

Sonoma Beach
Zinfandel
Sonoma County
ALCOHOL 13.5% BY VOLUME

Southern Right

PINOTAGE

1999

WESTERN CAPE

750ml A384 PRODUCE OF SOUTH AFRICA Alc. 14.0% Vol.

Southern Right

Southern Right Vineyard	South Africa

The Southern Right whale was close to extinction in 1986 when the International Whaling Commission voted for the current fragile whaling ban agreement. Every spring, the whales migrate to calve in the warm waters of Walker Bay, near the town of Hermanus, South Africa, known as the Whale Capital of the World.

On the hills above Hermanus are Southern Right's vineyards, a venture owned by Anthony Hamilton-Russell, famous for his iconic Burgundian-style Pinot Noirs and Chardonnays. Now Anthony intends to make Pinotage just as famous. "I believe so much in the potential of this variety," he told me.

For every bottle of Southern Right sold, the vineyard makes a donation to benefit Southern Right Whale Conservation.

Tasting Notes

This wine has a bright red color and a warm coconut nose. It's soft-bodied with light red currant flavors. It's beautifully balanced, with a long, lingering finish.

Spatzendreck

Delheim Wines	South Africa

Michael "Spatz" Sperling is one of the giants of South African wine, but he wasn't always so respected. More than fifty years ago, he arrived from his native Germany with just fifteen dollars in his pocket to work at his uncle's wine farm. His early attempts at winemaking were not always appreciated. Proudly pouring a glass for his friends, he later heard one bluntly remark, "It tastes like shit." Spatz redoubled his efforts, determined that one day the friend would drink his words, so to speak.

Spatz's nickname means *sparrow*, and *dreck* is slang for *shit*, hence the cheeky golden sparrow pictured on the label making a deposit into a cask of Spatzendreck.

Tasting Notes

Spatzendreck is a luscious, scented, late harvest, sweet dessert wine made from Chenin Blanc. I love sitting in Delheim's open-air restaurant on the slopes of the Simonsberg, gazing at Table Mountain in the distance, with an after-dinner glass of chilled Spatzendreck in my hand.

DELHEIM

Spatzendreck

LATE HARVEST

0.75ℓe   alc. 13% vol

PRODUCED AND BOTTLED BY DELHEIM WINES (PTY)LTD
"DRIESPRONG" KOELENHOF C.P. SOUTH AFRICA

PRODUCE OF SOUTH AFRICA

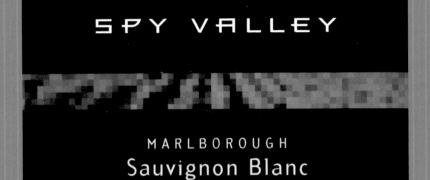

SPY VALLEY

MARLBOROUGH
Sauvignon Blanc
2004

WINE OF NEW ZEALAND
13.5% VOL 750 ML

Spy Valley

| Johnson Estate | New Zealand |

The vineyard image on the Spy Valley label is enlarged to show individual pixels. There's Morse code around the neck, and the back label looks like an index card. This unique design is a tongue-in-cheek reference to the nearby Waihopai satellite interception station, part of the global Echelon spy system of the U.S. government that uses receivers in huge golf-ball shaped domes to eavesdrop on electronic communications, including telephone calls, faxes, and e-mails.

Spy Valley is the local name for Wairau Valley, in New Zealand, where the Johnson Estate's 360 acres (145 hectares) of vineyards are planted with eight grape varieties on terraces above the Omaka River.

Tasting Notes

No place better expresses the character of Sauvignon Blanc than New Zealand, and this is a thumping good example, with beautifully delineated citrus, gooseberry, and new-mown grass flavors over crisp acidity with spicy tropical fruits and a lingering finish. A plate of fresh oysters would be a perfect accompaniment.

Star Galaxy Red

Summerhill Pyramid Winery	Canada

The Summerhill winery constructed a four-story high pyramid, made from dense concrete and aligned to the North Star, to age their wines. After fourteen years of comparative tastings, the winery is convinced that pyramid-aged wines taste smoother and have better aromas.

New York developer Stephen Cipes brought grape clones from France and "personally planted them on [his] hands and knees." Summerhill's forty-five acres (18 hectares) of vines form Canada's largest certified organic vineyard. The lack of herbicides and pesticides "keeps the lake clean, and our grapes don't taste of the chemicals," says Cipes, whose winery Mission Statement is "Divine purpose in every blessed drop."

This award-winning label is one of a series showing a couple driving to picnic in Summerhill's vineyards. Stickers on the car indicate the red is made from Cabernet Franc and Pinot Noir.

Tasting Notes

Pinot Noir gives a Burgundian feel to this wine, with some bright cherry flavors. Serve chilled with a picnic hamper of cold meats, cheeses, and crusty bread.

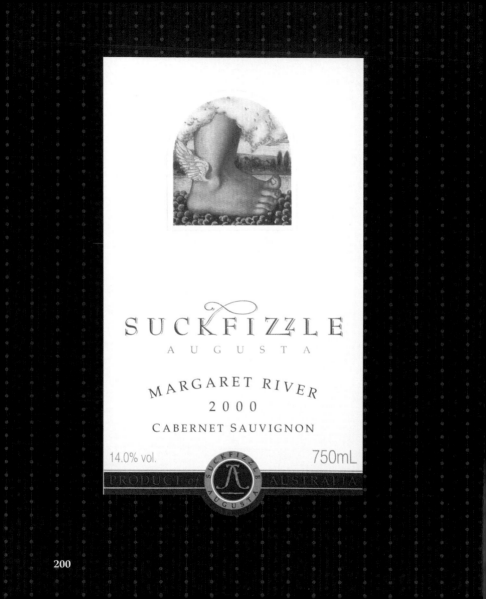

SUCKFIZZLE

AUGUSTA

MARGARET RIVER

2000

CABERNET SAUVIGNON

14.0% vol.

750mL

PRODUCT of AUSTRALIA

Suckfizzle

Stella Bella Wines	Australia

The Great Lord Suckfizzle is a character in the writings of François Rabelais, the sixteenth-century French monk, physician, and humorous writer. His bawdy tales of the giant Gargantua and his son Pantagruel delighted the populace, upset authorities, and inspired the name of a small vineyard in the cool maritime climate of the Margaret River region of Western Australia. The vineyard was named by winemaker Janice McDonald, who is a fan of Rabelais and wants to make wines with Rabelaisian style and flair.

So far Suckfizzle has produced two wines: a white blend of Sauvignon Blanc and Semillon and this 100% Cabernet Sauvignon. These are premium wines made from individually selected grapes.

Tasting Notes

The 2000 Cabernet Sauvignon was aged two years in oak barrels and has a beautiful, clear, ruby-red color and a rather subdued nose. It's well balanced with flavors of black currant, raspberry, and mint, integrated tannins, and a slightly smoky finish. This restrained, elegant wine is perfect with roasts or grilled meats.

Tex-Zin

| Messina Hof Wine Cellars | Texas |

Are you offended by Tex-Zin's label? Messina Hof's red Zinfandel uses an original work by Texan artist Emma Stark that depicts children in the vineyards. Seems harmless enough, and yet the winery received complaints about the shape of the folds in the middle child's clothing. On later vintages, this section of the painting was obscured by extra vine leaves.

Texas is the fifth largest wine-producing state in America. There are more than eighty-five wineries making excellent wines that locals keep to themselves; very little is seen outside the Lone Star state. Messina Hof, one of Texas's leading wineries, takes its name from the Sicilian town of Messina and the German town of Hof, which is where the families of owners Paul and Merrill Bonarrigo originated.

Tasting Notes

Tex-Zin (they say, "it's more than a big Zin, it's Texas sized") is a berry rich wine, with a good body, spices, and some soft tannins from aging in American oak. I've enjoyed this wine with thick, juicy, Texan beef cooked over mesquite, and it also suits Tex-Mex dishes. Yee-hahhh!

Messina Hof

TEXZIN
ZINFANDEL

TEXAS   Barrel Reserve   1997

RESERVE
VIOGNIER

Truck Stop Girl

Walker's Pass	California

Back in 1986, Viognier was so rare it wasn't even named in the French Agricultural Census. Only eighty acres (32 hectares) of the grape were planted in the whole world, nearly all in Condrieu, on the northern Rhône in France. These expensive wines had passionate devotees. Over the past twenty years, adventurous winemakers across the New World and in southern France planted the grape, not just for white wines but also to coferment it with red Syrah. When Chardonnay drinkers started looking for a change, Viognier—with its floral, honeyed apricot flavors and low acidity—took off.

Now Viognier has become widespread, prices have tumbled, and we are seeing bulk Viognier, like Truck Stop Girl. This wine from California's Central Valley was shipped in bulk to France, where it was bottled and given an evocative, American-looking label.

Tasting Notes

Truck Stop Girl Reserve Viognier is pale, with a green tinge and green grassy nose. It's light-bodied with some apricot flavors and a crisp finish that partners well with grilled lemon sole.

True Frogs

Black Sheep Vintners	California

Frogs are a popular motif on wine labels, and Black Sheep Vintners's amphibians have a unique literary connection to Calaveras County. Mark Twain stayed there in the mid-1800s while visiting the Sierra Nevada gold fields and wrote about Jim Smiley's celebrated jumping frog. Jim boasted his frog could catch flies on command, and he bet it would out-jump any frog in Calaveras County. A passing stranger showed interest, but regretted he didn't have a frog of his own.

Eager to take a bet, Jim went out to the swamp to catch a frog for him. When the two frogs were placed side by side, the new frog jumped, but Jim's wouldn't even move. The stranger pocketed his winnings and left. When Jim picked up his frog, he found it suspiciously heavy. On tipping it over, a hoard of lead shot poured out the frog's mouth, but Jim never caught up with the stranger.

Tasting Notes

This easy-drinking blend of Zinfandel and Cinsaut is light-bodied and bright-colored, with soft raspberry flavors and a hint of vanilla oak.

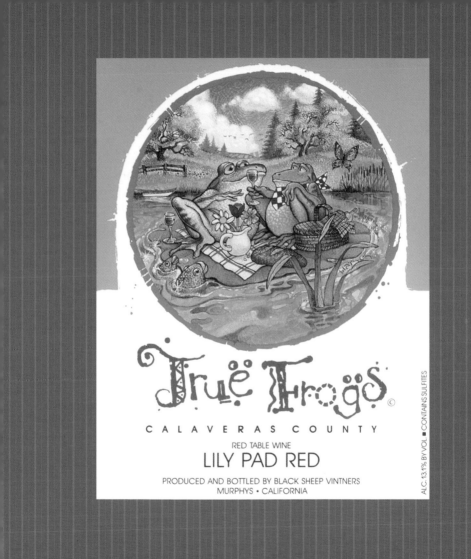

True Frogs ©

C A L A V E R A S   C O U N T Y

RED TABLE WINE
LILY PAD RED

PRODUCED AND BOTTLED BY BLACK SHEEP VINTNERS
MURPHYS • CALIFORNIA

ALC. 13.1% BY VOL. ■ CONTAINS SULFITES

PRODUCE OF SOUTH AFRICA

Under The Table

RUBY CABERNET / CINSAUT
Western Cape

13% vol   75cl ℮

Under the Table

Kingsland Wine & Spirits	South Africa

We've seen this traveler before, on labels for Hair of the Dingo (page 102) and Scraping the Barrel (page 177), and now he's journeyed to South Africa. "Under the table" is slang for having had a little too much to drink, but in this case it's clear from the picture that the table in question is Cape Town's huge flat-topped Table Mountain. The wine is an interesting blend of Ruby Cabernet and Cinsaut. Ruby comes from California; it's a 1930s cross of Cabernet Sauvignon and Carignan designed to deliver the quality of the first with the quantity of the second in the heat of Central Valley.

Few think that Ruby meets the first objective, but its great attribute, so growers tell me, is that the vines withstand strong winds and thus can be planted on exposed hills. Like most varieties, Ruby's quality depends on the care it receives in the vineyard and winery. Mostly we see it in a blend, as here.

Tasting Notes

This wine has a bright blue-purple color, with a juicy nose and a racy, fruity taste of red currants and raspberries. There's enough tannin backing to make this a good food match with bobotie, South Africa's sweetly spiced, baked, minced lamb curry.

The Unpronounceable Grape

Hilltop Neszmély | Hungary

This winery has made a virtue out of a name that few outside Hungary would attempt to pronounce. Cserszegi Füszeres is an attractive new Hungarian variety resulting from the recent crossing of local Irsai Olivér and world traveler Gewürztraminer. Apart from its name, this variety has a lot going for it, including fresh floral spiciness, good depth, and light alcohol. If you want to impress sommeliers, try saying *"chair-sheggy foo-share-us"* when ordering this varietal. It comes from award-winning winemaker Ákos Kamocsay at the ultra-modern Hilltop Neszmély winery.

Tasting Notes

This was my first experience of Cserszegi Füszeres, and I was delighted by its floral bouquet, which leads into easy drinking and dry, zingy spiciness with an underlying grapey ripeness. It is a great aperitif wine and good with scampi, broiled chicken breasts, or veal.

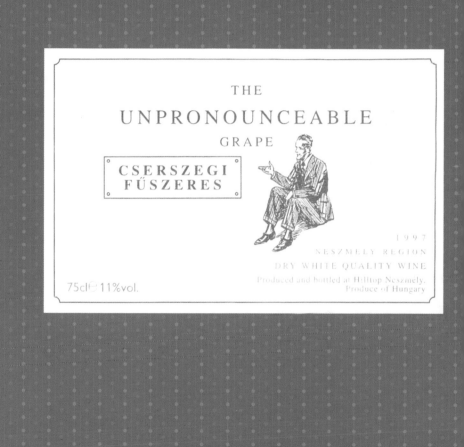

THE

UNPRONOUNCEABLE

GRAPE

CSERSZEGI
FŰSZERES

1997
NESZMELY REGION
DRY WHITE QUALITY WINE
Produced and bottled at Hilltop Neszmely.
Produce of Hungary

75cl ℮ 11%vol.

up a gum tree

SHIRAZ
SOUTH EASTERN
AUSTRALIA

PRODUCE OF AUSTRALIA

Up a Gum Tree

Vinocerous	Australia

Australian wines are on a roll. They've never been more popular with consumers, who appreciate their good taste, good value, and reliability. So when wine importer and distributor Vinocerous decided to ship and label its own range of Australian wines, it wanted a name that would clearly identify the contents as being from Down Under.

"Up a gum tree" is a well-known Australian phrase. It means being in a difficult position, stuck, or stranded. Add a picture of a colorful Ozzie bird up said tree and you have a label that screams "I'm Australian!" to passing consumers.

This particular wine is a Shiraz, the variety Australians have made their own. It originated in France's Rhône Valley, where it's known as Syrah. The grape was first planted in Australia in 1832 and in California in 1970. Whether called Syrah or Shiraz, this red grape is becoming a favorite throughout the world.

Tasting Notes

This is a full-bodied wine, richly flavored with black cherry and black currant. It has soft tannins and a warm finish.

Van Der Table

Vin de Table—table wine—is a simple, everyday, unfortified wine that hasn't attained any quality classification. Coming from a country where *Van der* is a frequently encountered surname prefix, and Table Mountain is a national icon, it's easy to see how the name of this table wine came about. What is harder to decode is the meaning of the picture. The man's head has proteas—South Africa's national flower—for ears. His brain is a bunch of grapes, being nibbled by a mouse. The head is on Bloubergstrand beach, with Table Mountain in the distance.

The wine itself is an Old Block red, meaning the grapes come from old planted vineyards. *Block* is also slang for *head*, but that doesn't really clear up very much. It might make more sense after you've poured yourself a few glasses.

Tasting Notes

The wine is made from Zinfandel, Ruby Cabernet, Cinsaut, Shiraz, Tinta Barocca, and Pinotage separately vinified by winemakers Frank Meeker, Eric Saayman, Gesie Lategan, and Graham Knox before blending. The result is an enjoyable, full-bodied drink, with dark fruit flavors—plums and berries—and enough tannins to give some backbone.

VAN ROUGE

Vin de Pays de Vaucluse

12.5% vol   75cl ℮

Mis en bouteille par
Du Peloux à Courthézon (Vaucluse), France
Produce of France

Van Rouge

Vignobles Du Peloux	France

The French call red wine *vin rouge* and pronounce it *van roozsh*. This simple wine is served in the local restaurants and bars of Avignon when the call goes out for a glass of house red. For export, they've cleverly punned the name with a picture of the red-paneled Citroën van used for local deliveries.

Vin de Pays is French for "country wines" and denotes the French government classification for wines that are better than ordinary, yet don't meet strict Appellation Contrôlée terms. Since one of those conditions restricts which grape varieties can be used, innovative producers who planted fashionable varieties and make excellent wines can sell them only as Vin de Pays. However, since Vin de Pays wines are allowed to name the variety on their label (which Appellation Contrôlée mostly cannot), this is a considerable advantage when exporting to countries that know little, and care even less, about French bureaucracy.

Tasting Notes

Van Rouge doesn't state a variety, but it's a pleasing drink, with some soft berry fruits, and would make a good partner to a hearty meat casserole.

Vous en Voulez, en Voilà

Domaine de Gravillas	France

Nicole and John Bojanowski built up a fan base with red wines made from their ninety-five-year-old Carignan vines. But customers kept asking when the vineyard's newly planted Syrah and Cabernet Sauvignon would be ready. The delay was due to Mother Nature; the surrounding wildlife kept destroying the harvest. The winemakers even tried electric fences, which were trampled down by leathery-skinned wild boars.

Clearly, more serious action was needed. So they blasted two hundred postholes into the underlying granite, dug a 738-yard (675-m) ditch, and erected a two-yard (2-m) high game fence in it. At last, they had enough grapes to make wine. All grapes are hand selected in the vineyards ("if it's not good enough to eat, we throw it away," says John) and then gently foot-crushed before fermentation.

This blend features equal measures of Syrah, Cabernet Sauvignon, and Carignan. The wine's name means, "You wanted it, you got it."

Tasting Notes

This is a rich, soft, warm, berry fruited wine, with sweet jammy blackberry flavors, some tannin structures, and a long aftertaste.

VOUS EN VOULEZ

EN VOILÀ

DOMAINE DE GRAVILLAS 2003
Vin de Pays des Côtes de Brian

Mis en Bouteille par
Nicole et John Bojanowski, Vignerons
34360 Saint-Jean-de-Minervois – France

13,5% vol. 750 ml   Produce of France
www.closdugravillas.com

FIREFINCH

GROWN WITH DEDICATION ... MADE WITH PASSION

WHAT THE BIRDS LEFT...
2002

RIPE RED

NAMED AFTER THE RAVENOUS FINCHES WHICH,
DRIVEN BY THEIR SUPERIOR SENSE OF SMELL AND TASTE,
DEVOUR THE GRAPES WHEN FULLY RIPE,
A TELLTALE SIGN THAT IT IS TIME TO PICK.

THIS WINE IS PACKED WITH CRUSHED RED PLUM
AND CHERRY FLAVOURS, JUICY AND LUSCIOUS IS THE FRUIT
FROM OUR SUN-DRENCHED VALLEY.

PRODUCED IN THE
WINE OF ORIGIN ROBERTSON
REGION OF
THE REPUBLIC OF SOUTH AFRICA

SOUTH AFRICAN
WINE

750ml

14,0% Vol.

6 007380 000228

BIBENDUM WINE LTD
113 REGENTS PARK ROAD
LONDON

L3287

What the Birds Left

Springfield Estate	South Africa

Many years ago on my first vineyard visit, standing in Bordeaux among rows of vines laden with plump grapes, I asked the vineyard owner whether he lost many grapes to birds. He looked at me as if I were mad and shrugged his shoulders. My guide explained that enthusiastic hunters blasted birdlife out of the air long before they could reach the vineyard. But birds are a problem in many other countries.

This wine ruefully tries to make the best of the situation. When local finches start swooping over the vineyard, it explains, the winemakers know it's time to begin picking. Springfield Estate is owned by brother and sister Abrie and Jeanette Bruwer, the fourth generation of winemakers on the farm. Abrie is a passionate and experimental winemaker who prefers to concentrate on the vineyard and to ferment using natural yeasts on the grape skins.

Tasting Notes

Firefinch is Springfield Estate's second label (see Glossary, page 247), and What the Birds Left is made from a blend of 50% Merlot, 30% Ruby Cabernet, and 20% Cabernet Sauvignon. It's a tremendously flavorsome big wine, packed with jammy ripe fruit and backed with firm tannins.

White Trash White

Oildale Winery	California

A home winemaker's joke turned into a business after a bottle donated to a charity auction raised $100. Old friends Terry Hill and Clete Harper first made their Red Neck Red from a kit, for themselves and friends. They then applied for a wholesale license and bought bottles of wine from a nearby winery, which they then labeled themselves.

A local store agreed to display a few bottles, and the press wrote about them. When the store called back and ordered a hundred cases, they knew they had a success. The original Red Neck Red and White Trash White were followed by Grandpa's Zinful Ways, Granny's Last Syrah, and Tiny Bubbles California Champagne.

The back label offers an amusing description of the vineyard: "Strategically planted between pumping oil wells and oil sumps are rows of grapevines. This blend of oil- and tar-tainted soils lends itself to a wine grape flavor seldom duplicated throughout the world of viticulture."

Tasting Notes

White Trash White Chardonnay is easy drinking on its own and ideal with fried catfish.

Harper Hill
FINE
WINE
Leslie Lou
White Trash White
TM
California Chardonnay
Distributed by
Harper Hill • Bakersfield, California
oildalewinery.com
750ml / Product of USA
Alcohol Vol. 12.5%

WILD CAT 2000

CATARRATTO

SICILIA

Indicazione Geografica Tipica

DA UVE DA AGRICOLTURA BIOLOGICA

FIRRIATO

WINE MADE FROM ORGANICALLY GROWN GRAPES

Wild Cat

Casa Vinicola Firriato	Italy

When Sicily's Firriato winery hired a group of Australian winemakers to introduce its New World techniques to the traditional Catarratto variety, the results paid off: Production expanded from four hundred thousand bottles in 1994 to more than four million in 2002, exported to more than thirty countries. Firriato grows traditional indigenous varieties such as Nero d'Avola, Perricone, and Grillo, as well as Catarratto (known among the Australians as *cat*).

Catarratto was once used to produce Marsala-fortified wines and was long considered to make a rather indifferent white wine in large quantities. But when treated seriously, with low yields and good winemaking, it produces a most enjoyable drink. This cat would be welcome in my home at any time.

Tasting Notes

This dry white wine comes from low-yielding bush vines in organically certified vineyards. It's a pale straw color, with a herby nose and crisp citrus flavors.

Winds of Change

African Terroir	South Africa

It's a rare wine that takes its name from a political speech. Addressing the parliament of 1960s apartheid South Africa, British Prime Minister Harold Macmillan said governments couldn't ignore African nationalism: "The most striking of all the impressions I have formed since I left London a month ago is the strength of the African consciousness. In different places it may take different forms, but it is happening everywhere. The wind of change is blowing through the continent." He also stated that Britain would not support apartheid.

Launched in 1999, Winds of Change funds social and economic black empowerment in the South African wine industry. Families living on the wine farm now own their houses and thirty acres (12 hectares) of land, which they farm. A portion of the profits of every bottle is contributed toward the community. With over 90 percent of the original objectives achieved, the project has expanded to include 250 workers at another farm.

Tasting Notes

Winds of Change is a complementary blend of Merlot and Pinotage; it offers smoky cherry and mulberry fruits with a tangy sweet finish. Ideal with braised lamb shanks.

WINDS OF CHANGE

Merlot Pinotage

WESTERN CAPE

2003

13.5%vol 75cl

PRODUCED AND BOTTLED
BY SONOP WINE FARM A991
PRODUCE OF SOUTH AFRICA

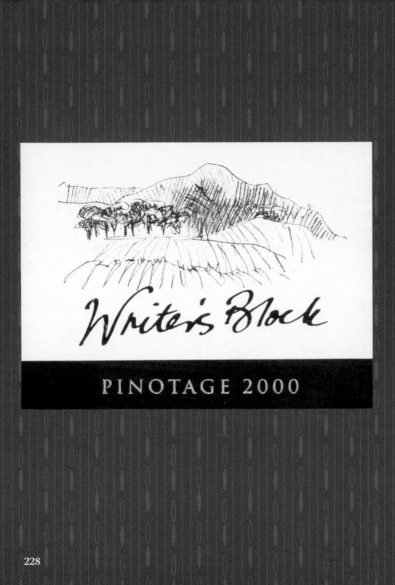

Writer's Block

PINOTAGE 2000

Writer's Block

Flagstone Winery	South Africa

Among winemakers and wine enthusiasts, a *block* refers to a small vineyard or a distinct group of rows in a large field. Many wine lovers prefer to buy wine with a sense of identity, and a single block wine is as geographically specific as you can currently get.

But when Flagstone wanted to make a single block Pinotage from a vineyard it leased some miles from the winery, it encountered a problem. The smallest area allowed to be identified on South African wine labels is an *estate*—a winery that makes wine only from its own surrounding vineyards.

Nevertheless, Bruce Jack, Flagstone's innovative winemaking owner, called the wine Writer's Block and submitted the name for registration. The authorities rejected it, citing the ban on identifying individual blocks. When Bruce went to an English dictionary to explain that writer's block is in fact a common author's malady, however, the name was approved.

Tasting Notes

Writer's Block is an intensely flavored, full-bodied wine, made from wild yeast fermented late-picked grapes. It tastes of blueberry, dark chocolate, plums, and toasty oak.

YN

Gnekow Family Winery	California

This witty label was the winning entry in a wine label design contest. Winemaker Rudy Gnekow told me: "We are a family-run winery, and we wanted to develop a product that was affordable, that delivered high quality, and created a unique 'point of difference' on the shelf. We held an internal contest and awarded a $2,000 prize for the cleverest label featuring the state of California on it."

The winning label—with its outline of California and *YN* in large letters—was an immediate success, selling more than four thousand cases in its first year. And no wonder, for who doesn't enjoy a glass of YN?

Red and white YNs have different-colored labels so customers can look at the bottle and instantly identify them. According to Rudy, "We felt the label differentiated us in the marketplace and also delivered a fun wine for people to drink gathered around the barbecue."

Tasting Notes

Pictured is the YN white label, which is a blend of Chardonnay, Chenin Blanc, and Symphony. The wine is pleasing, fruity, aromatic, and underpinned by oak.

Zingaro

Parducci Wine Estate	California

Zingaros were colorful, free-spirited gypsies who once roamed the Italian countryside. The old vines that produced this wine were planted by Italian immigrants on hillsides in Mendocino County, one of California's first wine grape growing regions.

The striking label illustration is by San Francisco artist Michael Schwab, well known for his Winter Olympics postage stamp design and Golden Gate National Monument posters.

I tasted Zingaro's first vintage at Parducci Estate. I was told the brand was being used to highlight wines made from the oldest vineyards, where small berries and low yields from free-standing vines give an additional intensity to California's heritage variety. There is 3% of Petite Sirah blended in, a variety that complements Zinfandel and adds complexity.

Tasting Notes

This wine is spicily fruity and redolent of plums and sweet blackberries. It has a warm dusting of black pepper over some smooth tannins.

Appendices

Buying the Wines

All the labels in this book come from wines that are, or have been, commercially available from supermarkets or wine stores or direct from wineries themselves. Not all the wines will currently be available in your locality.

Various names are used for particular batches of wines. Wine is a finite commodity. Less is made in poor years. In good years there will be excess, some of which may be sold under a name that lasts only as long as the surplus. For example, the French Appellation Contrôlée laws limit how much output a vineyard may produce. Wine above this amount cannot be sold as AC wine. Rather than pour the extra down the drain, a winery can sell it to a merchant who will invent a brand name and resell the wine to shops. But if the following year's harvest is poor, that brand name will probably vanish from shelves.

Some wines change names in different markets; for example, Britain's Old Git and Old Tart are both sold as Old Fart in the United States. The French wine Utter Bastard was marketed in the United States and United Kingdom as Fat Bastard Syrah. (As far as I know, both Rude Boy and Rude Girl are still waiting for an invite to cross the pond.)

The invaluable Wine Searcher Web site at www.wine-searcher.com lets you search for wines by name, vintage, and locality, listing prices and stocklists, and identifies sellers that will deliver. But if some of these labels are unavailable to you, it is certain that you can get some interesting labels that I cannot, and if you'd like to send them to me, I'd be delighted to add them to www.winelabels.org.

Winery Contact Details

Contact details for wines featured in the book are given on the following pages. Before traveling, you should phone ahead and make sure they still have the wines that interest you. More importantly, make sure they are open to visitors!

Telephone numbers are given in the international standard format. If phoning from outside the country of the address, replace the plus sign (+) with the international access code for the country you are calling from. For example, use 011 if you are in the United States and 00 if you are in a European Union country.

The digits immediately following + are the country code. Thus, if you phone Abbaye de Valmagne's number, +33 4 67 78 0609, from the United States, you would dial 011 33 4 67 78 0609.

If you are in the same country as the address you want to contact, dial that country's long-distance code instead of the country code. Thus, if you are in France, to call Abbaye de Valmagne you would simply dial 0 4 67 78 0609.

Abbaye de Valmagne
34560 Villeveyrac
France
+33 4 67 78 0609
www.valmagne.com

African Terroir
Sonop Wine Farm
Voorpaardeberg Road
Paarl
South Africa
+27 21 869 8103
www.african-terroir.co.za

Angove's PTY Ltd.
Bookmark Avenue
Renmark, SA 5341
Australia
+ 61 8 8580 3100
www.angoves.com.au

ASDA
ASDA House
Southbank
Great Wilson Street
Leeds LS11 5AD
England UK
+44 500 10055
www.asda.co.uk

Benton-Lane Winery
PO Box 99
23924 Territorial Hwy.
Monroe, Oregon 97456
+1 541 847 5792
www.benton-lane.com

Black Sheep Vintners
Main St & Murphys
   Grade Rd
Murphys, California 95247
+1 209 728 2157
www.blacksheepwinery.com

Blasted Church
378 Parsons Road
RR #1 S-32 C-67
Okanagan Falls
B.C. V0H 1R0
Canada
+1 250 497 1125
www.blastedchurch.com

Bodega Norton SA
Ruta Provincial 15, km 23.5,
Luján de Cuyo, Mendoza
Argentina
+54 261 490 9700
www.norton.com.ar

Bonny Doon Vineyards
10 Pine Flat Road,
Bonny Doon
Santa Cruz, California
   95061
+1 831 425 3625
www.bonnydoonvineyard.com

Brokenwood Wines
401–427 McDonalds Road
Pokolbin
NSW, Australia
+61 2 4998 7559
www.brokenwood.com.au

Bully Hill Vineyards
8843 Greyton H. Taylor
Memorial Drive
PO Box 458
Hammondsport, New York
14840-0458
www.bullyhill.com

Ca' del Solo
Santa Cruz
10 Pine Flat Road,
Bonny Doon
Santa Cruz
California 95061
+1 831 425 3625
www.cadelsolo.com

Cantina di Custoza
Località Staffalo 1
37060 Custoza
Verona
Italy
+39 045 516200
www.cantinadicustoza.it

Cantina di Montefiascone
Via Cassia 22
01027 Montefiascone (VT)
Italy
+39 0761 826148
www.cantinadimonte
   fiascone.it

Capricorn Wines
Brook House
4 Northenden Road
Gatley, Cheadle

Cheshire, SK8 4DN
England UK
+44 161 908 1314
www.capricornwines.co.uk

Carmenet Winery
This name is now owned by
Berringer Blass Wine Estates.
The original winery building is
owned by Chalone Wine Group
610 Airpark Road
PO Box 4500
Napa, California 94558
+1 707 259 4500
www.carmenetwinery.com

Casa Vinicola Carlo Botter
Cadorna, 17
Fossalta di Piave
Italy
+39 4 216 7194
www.botter.it

Casa Vinicola Firriato
Via Trapani, 4
91027, Paceco
Sicily, Italy
+39 923 882755
www.firriato.it

Chalone Wine Group
621 Airport Road
Napa, California 94558
+1 707 254 4200
www.chalonewinegroup.com

Cheers Wine & Beers
Z.A. Marcel Doret

199 Rue Marcel Doret
62100 Calais
France
+33 32 119 7700
www.cheers.fr

Cleavage Creek Cellars
PO Box 1798
Windsor, California 95492
+1 707 836 8602
www.cleavagecreek.com

Click Wine Group
808 Howell Street
5th Floor
Seattle, Washington 98101
+1 206 443 1996
www.clickwinegroup.com

**Confrerie de Vignerons
de Oisly et Thésée**
Le Bourg 41700
Oisly
France
+33 02 5479 7520

**Co-operative Group
(CWS) Ltd**
Manchester
M60 4ES
England UK
+44 800 0686 727
www.co-op.co.uk

**Coopers Creek
Vineyard**
PO Box 140

Kumea, Auckland
New Zealand
+64 9 412 8560
www.cooperscreek.co.nz

CPS SRL
Centro Produzione
Spumanti Srl
Via Moronico 38
48010 Marzeno di
Brisighella (RA)
Italy
+39 546 40196
www.cpsspumanti.it

Delheim Wines
PO Box 10
Koelenhof
7605, South Africa
+27 21 888 4600
www.delheim.com

DLM Wines
999 Foreman Lane
Healdsburg
California 95448
+1 707 433 3711
www.dlmwine.com
www.pinupwine.com

Domaine de Gravillas
34360
Saint Jean de Minervois
France
+33 46 738 1752
www.closdugravillas.com

Domaines Paul Mas
Château de Conas
34120 Pézenas
France
+33 46 790 1610
www.paulmas.com

Domaine Vistalba
Roque Saenez Peña
s/n Vistalba (5507)
Lujan de Cuyo, Mendoza
+54 261 498 2330

Durney Vineyards
Heller Estate
PO Box 999
69 W. Carmel Valley Road
Carmel Valley, California
93924
+1 831 659 6220
www.hellerestate.com

EastEnders
14 rue Gustave Courbet
62100 Calais
France
+33 321 345333
www.eastenders-calais.com

Envoy Wines
London SW19 8UG
England UK

**Fat Bastard Wine Company
(UK)**
See Guy Anderson Wines

**Fat Bastard Wine Company
(US)**
Click Wine Group
808 Howell Street
5th Floor
Seattle, Washington 98101
+1 206 443 1996
www.fatbastardwine.com

Ferlandia Predappio
Via Roma 100
Predappio FC
Italy
+39 543 92 3335
www.ferlandia.com

Flagstone Winery
P O Box 3636
Somerset West, 7130
South Africa
+27 21 852 5052
www.flagstonewines.com

Freie Weingärtner Wachau
A-3601 Dürnstein
Austria
+43 2711 371
www.fww.at

Gnekow Family Winery
17347 East Gawne Road
Collegeville, California
95215
+1 888 446-3569
www.gnekow.com

Graceland Cellars
2536 Barrington Court
Hayward, California
94545
+1 877 499 4637
www.gracelandcellars.com

Gundlach Bundschu Winery
2000 Denmark Street
Sonoma, California 95476
+1 707 938 5277
www.gunbun.com

Guy Anderson Wines
Roundham House
Oxen Road
Crewkerne
Somerset TA18 7HN
England
+44 1460 271670

Hatten Wines
Jl. Danau Tondano
Sanur, Denpasar
Bali
Indonesia 80228
+62 361 286298
www.hattenwines.com

Heller Estate
PO Box 999
69 W. Carmel Valley Road
Carmel Valley,
California, 93924
+1 831 659 6220
www.hellerestate.com

Hilltop Neszmély
1024 Budapest
Ady Endre u. 11-13
Hungary
+36 1 336 22 20
www.hilltop.hu

Houghton Wine Company
Dale Road, Middleswan
Western Australia 6056
Australia
+61 8 9274 9550
www.houghton-wines.com.au

HRM Rex-Goliath Wines
PO Drawer C
37700 Foothill Rd
Soledad, California 93960
+1 831 678 2132
www.rexgoliath.com

International Wine Services
Punchbowl Park
Cherry Tree Lane
Hemel Hempstead
HP2 7EU
England UK
+44 144 220 6800
www.wine-info.co.uk

J. L. Terrier & C. Collovray
F-71960 Davayé
Mâconnais
France
+33 38 535 8651

Johnson Estate Limited
RD6 Waihopai Valley Road
Marlborough
New Zealand
+64 3 572 9840
www.spyvalleywine.co.nz

Kingsland Wine & Spirits
The Winery
Fairhills Road, Irlam
Manchester, M44 6BD
England UK
+44 161 333 4300
www.kingsland-wines.com

Lacheteau S.A.
Z.I. de la Saulaie
49700 Doue-la-Fontaine
France
+33 2 4159 2626

L. Mawby Vineyards
4519 S Elm Valley Rd
Suttons Bay
Michigan 49682
+1 231 271 3522
www.lmawby.com

MadFish Wines
Scotsdale Road
Denmark, WA 6333
Australia
+61 8 9848 2345
www.madfishwines.com.au

Maison Coquard
Hameu "Le Boiter"
69620 Theize en Beaujolais

France
+33 47 471 1159
www.maison-coquard.com

M. Chapoutier
18 Avenue Dr Paul Durand
B. P. 38 - 26601 TAIN
Cedex
France
+33 475 082 865
www.chapoutier.com

Messina Hof Wine Cellars
4545 Old Reliance Road
Bryan, Texas 77808
+1 409 778 9463
www.messinahof.com

Milano Family Winery
14594 South Highway 101
Hopland, California 95449
+1 800 5642582
www.milanowinery.com

Muratie Estate
PO Box 133
Koelenhof 7605
South Africa
+27 21 865 2330
www.muratie.co.za

Nova Wines
PO Box 1014
St Helena, California 94574
+1 707 963 5475
www.marilynwines.com

Oddbins Limited
31–33 Weir Road
Wimbledon SW19 8UG
England UK
+44 800 917 4093
www.oddbins.com

Oildale Winery
4800 Stockdale Highway
    Ste 304
Bakersfield, California
93309
+1 661 397 3603
www.oildalewinery.com

Paddagang Vignerons
21 Church Street
Tulbagh
South Africa
+27 23 230 0242
www.tulbagh.net/paddagang.htm

Parducci Wine Estate
501 Parducci Road
Ukiah, California 95482
+1 877 946 4276
www.zingaro.net

Paul Boutinot (UK)
Brook House
4 Northenden Road
Gatley, Cheadle
Cheshire, SK8 4DN
+44 161 908 1300
www.boutinot.com

Paul Boutinot Wine Estates Inc (US)
9 Tanglewood Drive
East Hanover, New Jersey
07936
+1 973 599 1730
www.boutinotwine.com

Peter Lehmann Wines
Off Para Road
Tanunda
SA 5253
Australia
www.peterlehmannwines.com

Ridge Vineyards
17100 Monte Bello Road
Cupertino, California 95014
+1 408 867-3233
www.ridgewine.com

Sakonnet Vineyards
162 West Main Rd
Little Compton, Rhode
Island 02837
+1 800 919 4637
www.sakonnetwine.com

Salt Spring Vineyards
151 Lee Road at the
    1700 block
Fulford Ganges Rd
Salt Spring Island, BC
Canada V8K 2A5
+1 250 653 9463
www.saltspringvineyards.com

Seppelt & Sons Limited
403 Pacific Highway
Artarmon NSW 2064
Australia
+61 2 9465 1000
www.seppelt.com.au

Sharpe Hill Vineyard
108 Wade Road
Pomfret, Connecticut 06258
+1 860 974-3549
www.sharpehill.com

Southern Right Vineyard
PO Box 158
Hermanus, 7200
South Africa
+27 28 312 3595

Stella Bella Wines
Gnarawary Road
Margaret River
WA 6285
Australia
+61 8 9757 6377
www.stellabella.com.au

Stu Pedasso Cellars
5700 Gravenstein Highway
North
Forestville, California 95436
+1 800 8676567
www.stupedasso.com

Summerhill Pyramid Winery
4870 Chute Lake Road
Kelowna

British Columbia V1W
4M3
Canada
+1 250)764-8000
www.summerhill.bc.ca

Swartland Winery
PO Box 95
Malmesbury, 7299
South Africa
+27 22 482 1134
www.swwines.co.za

Tait Wines
Yaldara Drive
Lyndoch, 5351
Australia
+61 8 85 245000
www.taitwines.com.au

Terraustral
Hernando de Aguirre 1915
Santiago, Chile
Tel: +56 2 679 0600
arubio@terraustral.cl

Three Choirs Vineyards
Newent
Gloucestershire GL18 1LS
England UK
+44 1531 890223
www.three-choirs-vineyards.co.uk

**Three Loose Screws
Wine Company**
PO Box 1248
Sonoma
California 95476

+1 707 933 1704
www.3loosescrews.com

Toad Hollow Tasting Room
409A Healdsburg Avenue
Healdsburg, California
95448
+1 707 431 8667
www.toadhollow.com

Two Hands Wines
Neldner Road
Marananga
Barossa Valley S.A 5355
Australia
+61 8 8568 7900
www.twohandswines.com

Vernaux Noémie
3 Rue Verottes
21200
Beaune
+33 38 024 5401

Vignobles Du Peloux
Route d'Orange
84350 Courthézon
France
+33 49 070 4200
www.vignoblesdupeloux.com

Vinicola Cantele S.R.L.
Via Vincenzo Balsamo
13–73100 Lecce
Italy
+39 832 705010
www.cantele.it

Vinoceros
Stanley Way
Cardrew, Redruth
Cornwall, TR15 1SP
England, UK
+44 1209 314 711
www.vinoceros.com

Walker's Pass
Orbital Wines Ltd
13 Chapter Street,
London, SW1P 4NY
England UK
+44 207 802 5415

Waverley Vintners
2–4 Broadway Park
South Gyle Broadway
Edinburgh EH12 9JZ
Scotland
+44 131 528 1500
www.waverley-group.co.uk

Western Wines
1 Hawksworth Road
Central Park, Telford
Shropshire, TF2 9TU
England UK
+44 1952 235 700
www.western-wines.com

Wines of Charles Back
PO Box 583
Suider Paarl
7624
South Africa
+27 21 863 2450
www.fairview.co.za

There are four basic methods for removing wine labels from bottles. You can use

• heat to melt the adhesive
• liquid to dissolve the adhesive
• a blade to cut through the adhesive
• a clear adhesive-backed sheet to lift the label from its backing

The first two options will be successful if the label is self-adhesive. The third option works with all labels but requires a steady hand and a willingness to use a razor-sharp blade. The last is successful, but expensive, and although the label image is preserved, it is forever saved under clear plastic.

Heat

Nearly all New World wineries use self-adhesive labels, and this adhesive can usually be softened long enough to peel off the labels. If the information on the front of the bottle is split over more than one piece of paper—for instance, if the wine's name is on one label, a picture on a second, and the variety and vintage on a third—they're almost certain to be self-adhesive. Labels on old bottles and from Old World countries that look and feel like paper could well be loosened with liquid, but it's best to try heat first, as soaking can sometimes damage a label.

This is the method that works for me most times and the first one I try. Place the bottle upright in a sink or bowl and pour boiling water into the bottle to a depth above the label. The water must be as close to boiling as possible; I use an electric kettle and pour in the water just after the kettle automatically switches off. A funnel would be useful if you don't have a good pouring spout.

Leave for five minutes. Protect one hand with a cloth or oven mitt and steady the bottle by gripping its neck. With your other hand, slip a fingernail under the corner of the back label and see if it can be lifted. If it can, carefully peel off the back label. If the back label can be removed, so can the front label. The removed labels will be sticky; I affix them to a clean sheet of paper.

Alternatives to boiling water: I have successfully heated bottles for ten minutes in an oven set to 300°F (150°C). When traveling, I have sometimes used a hotel hairdryer, at its highest setting, directed on the label (unfortunately, I have no other use for hairdryers these days). Holding the bottle in the steam from a boiling kettle can work, but it is easy to scald oneself.

Soaking

If heat doesn't work, try soaking. Leaving the hot water inside the bottle, fill the sink or bowl with hot water from the tap until the label is covered. Either the label will float off on its own, or you can try gently peeling it after thirty minutes. Take care, as the label can start to disintegrate.

To avoid wasting hot water, I use a two-liter soda bottle with the top cut off. A wine bottle fits neatly in this with enough room for water around it.

Some people recommend adding wallpaper removal agents or other chemicals to the water, but my experiments have not been successful; the label will come off but it will be destroyed in the process. I suspect this advice comes from home winemakers who want a clean, reusable bottle instead of a well-preserved label.

Cutting

You need a thin, sharp, flexible edge—a razor blade is ideal. Make slicing movements with the blade at a low angle pointing down and touching glass. Cut through the adhesive while holding up the part of the label that is separated. Good results can be achieved with this method, although metallic print can be damaged, and finger cuts are a risk. The best way is to presoak plain paper labels for about an hour before cutting. For glossy or self-adhesive labels, put about an inch (2.5 cm) of hot water in the bottle and lay it on its side with the label at the bottom for about five minutes to help soften the glue before cutting.

Label Strippers

If the above methods fail, then I use a self-adhesive plastic sheet to remove labels. Several brands are commercially available. These sheets will literally strip the front of the label, with the image, from its backing—so the adhesive needs to be very strong. In my experience, the plastic adhesive sheets sold to cover books are not strong enough to work effectively.

The best method is to run a fingernail under one vertical edge of the label, raising it slightly. Next, remove the adhesive sheet from its backing and smooth it carefully across the label. I use the back of a dinner spoon to ensure a good seal.

Instructions that come with the sheets are wildly optimistic about how easy and quickly they work, implying the label will magically lift off within minutes. The adhesive actually needs time to make a strong bond, and the longer you can leave it in place—for a couple of days, if possible—the more success you will have.

When you peel off the sheet, start from the edge where you ran your fingernail under the label. Very slowly, start peeling. If some of the label doesn't come up, stop and firmly rub the sheet down onto it again. Wait before attempting to remove it again.

This method is the most expensive; a pack of ten sheets costs about $10 in the United States, £10 in UK, but it should save your most stubborn labels.

Alternatives

Photographing labels on the bottle is a way to keep a copy of the image without the hassle of removing the label. Others will use a digital scanner. To achieve the best results, rotate the bottle in time with the moving part of the scanner that captures the image.

Winery tasting rooms may have spare unused labels for collectors. You can usually get one or two just by asking. Most wineries are reluctant to part with more, as there is the risk of scammers sticking them on inferior wines. For this reason, certain premium wineries use labels that cannot be removed without damage.

Label Removing Resources

Label Lifters
1459 Gregory Rd.
R. R. #3,
St. Catharines
Ontario L2R 6P9
Canada
+1 905 7080159
www.vna.on.ca

Label Off
Oenophilia, Inc.
500 Meadowland Drive
Hillsborough, NC
27278
+1 919 644 0555
www.oenophilia.com

**Wine Appeal
Label Removers**
19 Davies Street
Safety Beach
Vic 3836
Australia
+61 3 5987 3483
www.wineappeal.com

**Wine Appeal Products
(USA)**
670 San Miguel Canyon
Road
Royal Oaks, CA 95076
+1 831 724 7688
www.wineappeal.com

Label Remover Suppliers
Label Library
Elvaston Group
9 Elvaston Mews
London SW7 5HY
England
+44 0207 581 4178
www.noblemacmillan.co.uk

Glossary

ABV: Alcohol by volume. The alcoholic content must be shown on the label of most wines.

AC: *See* Appellation Contrôlée

Advanced Tasting Program: A mail-order wine club operated by Ridge Winery to sell wines made in too small quantities for distribution through its normal outlets. Other wineries have similar programs.

Alcohol and Tobacco Tax and Trade Bureau: The Alcohol and Tobacco Tax and Trade Bureau (TTB) is the division of the United States Department of the Treasury responsible for regulation and taxation of wine. Labels for wines sold in the United States have to be submitted for prior approval to the TTB. Until January 2003 it was called the Bureau of Alcohol, Tobacco, and Firearms (BATF). The TTB Web site is www.ttb.gov.

Appellation Contrôlée: Appellation d'Origine Contrôlée is the highest level of French wine law classification that specifies, among other things, permitted grape varieties and output for the specific area covered by the appellation.

ATP: *See* Advanced Tasting Program

Back Label: A secondary label originally used to show additional marketing information about the wine. Increasingly, it is used to hold all the legally required information in order to free the front label for artwork.

Basket Pressed: Sometimes noted on labels to indicate a hands-on approach to winemaking. The basket is a circular bin made of upright wooden slats with spaces between them. Grapes are inserted and then a flat disc is placed on top and forced down with a hand-turned screw. One winemaker told me it was a very gentle way of pressing grapes, but another winemaker said he used it because he could "squeeze the shit out of them."

Blend: Usually used to mean a wine made from more than one variety. Blending varieties is normal practice in many regions, including Bordeaux and Rioja. Usually varieties are vinified separately then blended to achieve the desired final wine. However, even single variety wines are usually the result of blending wines from different vineyards, blocks, and barrels.

Bouquet: The smell given off from a wine. Glasses that curve inward at the top help to concentrate a wine's perfume. An unclean or moldy smell is the first indication of a bad wine.

Bureau of Alcohol, Tobacco, and Firearms: *See* Alcohol and Tobacco Tax and Trade Bureau

Bush Vines: Grape vines grown unsupported. They look like thigh-high bushes. The vine is stressed, which restricts growth and output. These vines cannot be machine harvested, and the words *bush vines* on a label often signify vines planted a long time ago.

Case: Twelve 75 cl bottles, equaling 9 liters. The introduction of easier-to-carry six-bottle packages caused confusion after some started calling such packages *cases*; when you see wine advertised "by the case," be sure to ascertain how many bottles are actually included.

Clone: Grape vines are always propagated by taking cuttings, rather than planting grape seeds. Sometimes one particular vine in a field will be superior, maybe through mutation or resistance to viruses, and will be chosen as the source for cuttings. All descendents of the original "mother vine" are genetically identical, but over centuries of selection, distinctly different clones appear, offering various advantages, and vineyards can choose which to plant.

Cross: The grape vine resulting from the breeding of two varieties from the same species. Thus Pinotage is a cross, as both its parents are vinifera (Pinot Noir and Cinsaut). *See also* Hybrid.

Dry: The opposite of sweet. A totally dry wine will not have any residual sugar, but an acidic wine can taste dry even when it does have some sugar. Tannins also give the impression of dryness. Nearly all red wines are dry. White wines can range from dry to sweet, and the label usually indicates how dry or sweet one is. Champagne uses the words *Brut Nature, Brut, Sec, Demi-Sec,* and *Doux* to indicate the range from driest to sweetest.

e: An e-mark on labels signifies the bottle conforms to the European Union average packing system. The EU approves only certain sized containers for wine; the standard wine bottle is 75 cl.

Enological: To do with wine and winemaking. From *oinos,* the Greek word for wine.

Fortified: A wine that has had spirits—usually brandy—added to prevent fermentation. Adding brandy during or before fermentation causes fermentation to cease before all the grape sugar is converted to alcohol. Fortification is used to make sweet wines. Examples of fortified wines are Port and Sherry.

Front Label: The main label for a wine, it faces outward on a store shelf and is intended to catch the consumer's eye. Many consumers make their buying choice based on the label, and the label is critically important to the wine's success. Increasingly, legally required information that used to be shown here is being moved to the back label so that the front label can make an impression.

Hybrid: In wine terms, *hybrid* has derogatory overtones and means a variety that is not pure vinifera. A hybrid is the result of a crossing between two different vine species, usually vinifera and native American varieties. Wines made from hybrids often inherit the damp, wool, "foxy" taste of the American variety. Hybrids are not normally allowed to be planted in the EU, and cannot be used in EU quality wines. They are widely used in many American states where conditions are too severe for vinifera, and hybrid varieties such as Baco Noir, Chambourcin, Vidal, and Vignoles make good wines.

IGT: An abbreviation for Indicazione Geografica Tipica. This is an Italian classification for basic country wines, one step up from a Vino da Tavola, or table wine.

Label: Labels on bottles are relatively new. They began to appear widely in the later half of the 1800s. They are a legal requirement on commercially sold wines and must contain certain information, such as the brand name, bottler, and alcohol content. National authorities and international agreement dictate what information must be shown, along with the size and positioning of the text and much more. The rules are complex and confusing: Wines sold in the United States must carry a government health warning, but this warning must *not* be shown on wines sold in the European Union. A varietal wine should contain at least 75% of that variety in the United States (or 51% of native vitis labrusca), but a minimum of 85% of the named variety is required in the EU. Professional Friends of Wine has an excellent description of wine labeling regulations at www.winepros.org/consumerism/labels.htm.

Lees: Sediment of dead yeast cells formed after fermentation.

Nose: The smell of a wine—*see* Bouquet. The term comes from the act of pushing one's nose deep into a tasting glass.

Phylloxera: An aphid that burrows into the roots of vines and kills them. There is no cure, and this little creature almost wiped out the world's vinifera vines in the late 1800s. Phylloxera is endemic in America; over millennia, surviving native vines developed a resistance to it. International trading of vines transmitted phylloxera worldwide, and nowadays vinifera vines are grafted onto resistant American rootstock almost everywhere.

Rootstock: The part of a vine with roots, onto which is grafted the upper part of a vinifera vine. Rootstocks are bred from native American vines selected primarily for their resistance to phylloxera.

Second Label: A second label is a brand name used by a winery for wines that it doesn't want to sell under its main brand name. Sometimes second label wines are from grapes not considered good enough for the main label, such as those from young vines that have not yet developed sufficient flavor. Second label wines are also used by wineries to increase production above what their own vineyards can grow by using bought-in grapes.

Shipper's Label: A wine brand name and label exclusive to a wine shipper rather than the winery that made it. Shippers either contract a winery to make a blend to their choice, bottle, and label it, or they'll import the wine in bulk and bottle and label it themselves locally. The source of the wine under a shipper's label could change from year to year, and the shipper could sell the same wine but with different labels to different markets.

Sulfites: Sulfite is an inclusive term for various forms of sulfur. Wines sold in the United States must state they contain sulfites when there's more than ten parts per million (ppm). All wine contain sulfites in some form because they are a byproduct of fermentation. Sulfur has been indispensable in winemaking since antiquity as a disinfectant and preservative, killing bacteria and wild yeasts, and it encourages fermentation and assists color and flavor extraction. Without use of sulfur, wine would be at risk of damage from bacteria, wild yeast, and oxidation.

Sur Lie: A French term for wine that has been left on its lees after fermentation. Leaving wine in contact with the lees increases flavor complexity.

Table: A non-fortified wine meant for drinking with a meal. Has a legal meaning in many countries; in the EU it is used for wines that do not meet a superior quality classification such as VdP or AC. In the United States, an alcohol level from 7 percent to 14 percent needn't be shown on the label if "Table Wine" is used instead. This means that a winemaker can use the same label every year without having to submit it for reapproval, even if the alcohol level has changed.

Tannins: Tannins are responsible for a firm, bitter taste, similar to strong black tea, that dries out the mouth. They act as a preservative and soften as wine ages, so wines made for long keeping might be unpleasant when young. Tannins come from the seeds, stems, and skins of grapes, thus white wines have fewer tannins, as their skins are discarded at the beginning, and some varieties have higher levels of tannins than others. Tannins also come from wood and are added by barrel fermenting and aging. Tannins give wines a backbone, help them to stand up to food, and add complexity.

TTB: *See* Alcohol and Tobacco Tax and Trade Bureau

Ungrafted: A vinifera vine that has not been grafted onto American rootstock. There are some locations that are free from phylloxera, including Chile and a few vineyards planted on sand (which seems to be a barrier to the aphid).

Varietal: Refers to a wine made from a named grape variety.

Variety: An individual type of grape vine within a species. Thus Merlot and Chardonnay are vinifera varieties.

VdP: Vin de Pays is the lowest layer in the French geographical wine classification system. It is sometimes used for wines that aren't allowed AC classification because they fall foul of rules on permitted varieties. VdP wines are allowed to specify the grape variety used—a bonus when selling in a world market that prefers to buy by variety.

Vinifera: *See Vitis Vinifera*

Vitis: The genus of plants that includes grape vines. There are more than sixty Vitis species native to America and Asia, and one native to Europe. The European Vinifera species is the primary wine-producing grape.

Vitis Labrusca: An American Vitis species. Concord (used for wine, grape juice, and jelly) is the most famous variety.

Vitis Vinifera: The wine-producing species of *Vitis*. Only the European Vinifera is considered to produce quality wine, and this has been planted everywhere wine is made. All the famous varieties (Cabernet, Pinot, Chardonnay, Merlot, Pinotage, Shiraz, etc.) are *Vinifera*.

Odd Facts

Haven't had your full of weird or obscure wine trivia? Here are a few more odd facts to send you on your way.

When visiting Muratie Estate in South Africa, you can actually spend the night in George Paul Canitz's studio, where the artist painted the portrait that appears on Amber Forever! (page 17). Book with the winery.

The first vintage of The Ball Buster (page 25) almost never made the market after a tanker tipped and the wine poured onto the ground.

Gundlach-Bundschu produces a white wine version of Bearitage (page 30) that features a polar bear on the label.

Big House Red 2001 (page 34) was a blend of 20% Syrah, 15% Cabernet Franc, 14% Carignane, 11% Sangiovese, 9% Barbera, 7% Petite Sirah, 5% Petite Verdot, 4% Grenache, 3% Old Vine Mourvedre, 3% Dolcetto, 2% Nebbiolo, 2% Zinfandel, 2% Charbono, 2% Cinsaut, 1% Viognier, 1% Riesling, 1% Mixed Red, 1% Miscellaneous.

Todd Williams, the co-owner of Toad Hollow and creator of Cacophony (page 49), is the half-brother of actor Robin Williams.

When Jeff Conner of Cleavage Creek (page 65) isn't making wine, he's busy at his day job, flying passenger jumbo jets for United Airlines.

Still worried that a Lazy Lizard (page 113) might end up in your wine glass? Take comfort from knowing that more and more wineries are installing sorting tables where grapes can be inspected before crushing. If any lizards did get caught by a harvester, they'd be saved at this point.

The blend of Love My Goat (page 117) changes from year to year and is said to contain one or more of the following hybrids: Aurora Blanc, Seyval Blanc, Ravat Blanc, Vidal Blanc, Verdelet Blanc, Rosette, Baco Noir, Cascade Noir, Chancellor Noir, Chelois Noir, Colobel Noir, Rougeon Noir, and Marechal Foch. All are grown in the Hammondsport area by Bully Hill.

Phoenix (page 145) isn't the only wine made from a new variety that was released in the past decade. Others include South Africa's Roobernet (a cross of Cabernet Sauvignon and Pontac), France's Marselan (Cabernet Sauvignon and Grenache) and New York's Chardonel (Seyval Blanc and Chardonnay).

Fair Dinkum—the name of the winery "responsible" for producing Sheila's Chardonnay (page 185)—is also an Australian term meaning "fair play," or "reliable and genuine."

The bird on the label of Smoking Parrot (page 189) was named Icarus by artist Ralph Steadman.

The people at Spy Valley (page 197) are looking forward a couple of years to when they'll be labeling their wines vintage 007.

Calaveras County, California, home of True Frogs (page 206), has held an annual Jumping Frog Jubilee in May since 1928. Last year, more than two thousand frogs participated. See www.frogtown.org.

Acknowledgments

Thanks to the following for helping to make this book possible:

Guy Anderson, John Bojanowski, Jeff Conners, Robin Garr, Rudy Gnekow, Bernie Hadley-Beauregard, Terry Hill, Annette Jacobs, Jonathan Kinns, Jim LaMar, Debbie Marion, Lorne Mews, Dennis De La Montanya, Angelo Musanti, Charlotte O'Beirne, John Palmer, Adam La Pierre, Deanna Starr, Jenise Stone, Tambi Schweizer, Michelle Tait, Todd Williams, Heather Wallace, Clare Wood.

Special thanks to my editors, Jason Rekulak and Erin Slonaker, designer Karen Onorato, and the rest of the Quirk Books team.

Also many thanks to all the artists, designers, technicians, and printers who produced the labels featured in this book.